'THE TRIUMPH OF LOVE

by Pierre Carlet de Chamblain de Marivaux

Adaptation by Stephen Wadsworth

B—
Stephen ——

SAMUEL FRENCH, INC.
45 WEST 25TH STREET   NEW YORK 10010
7623 SUNSET BOULEVARD HOLLYWOOD 90046
LONDON   TORONTO

FOR ANNE ROY

**With loving thanks to
Emily Mann, Janice Paran and
Nadia Benabid.**

IMPORTANT BILLING AND CREDIT REQUIREMENTS

All producers of THE TRIUMPH OF LOVE *must* give credit to the Author of the Play in all programs distributed in connection with performances of the Play and in all instances in which the title of the Play appears for purposes of advertising, publicizing or otherwise exploiting the Play and/or a production. The name of the Author *must* also appear on a separate line, on which no other name appears, immediately following the title, and *must* appear in size of type not less than fifty percent the size of the title type.

In addition the following credit must appear in all programs and advertising in connection with a performance of the Play:

> "This adaptation of THE TRIUMPH OF LOVE was originally commissioned and produced by McCarter Theatre, Princeton, New Jersey."

The Triumph of Love was played for the first time by the Comédie Italienne in Paris, March 12, 1732. This adaptation was originally commissioned and produced by the McCarter Theatre in Princeton, NJ, March 27, 1992, with the following cast and creative contributors:

LÉONIDE ....Katherine Borowitz
CORINE............................... Brooke Smith
HARLEQUIN.................John Michael Higgins
DIMAS...................................Tom Brennan
AGIS.................................... Mark Deakins
LÉONTINE .... Mary Lou Rosato
HERMOCRATE...................Robin Chadwick

Director ....Stephen Wadsworth
Set Designer........................... Thomas Lynch
Costume Designer ....Martin Pakledinaz
Lighting Designer..............Christopher Akerlind
Production Stage Manager.............Susie Cordon

Artistic Director, McCarter Theatre... Emily Mann
Assistant to Artistic Director..........Loretta Greco
Dramaturg ....Janice Paran

v

CHARACTERS

LÉONIDE, a princess (in disguise as Phocion, also uses the name Aspasie)

CORINE, her maid (in disguise as Hermidas)

HARLEQUIN, Hermocrate's valet

DIMAS, Hermocrate's gardener

AGIS, a prince and Hermocrate's ward

LÉONTINE, Hermocrate's sister

HERMOCRATE, a philosopher

The action takes place in the gardens of Hermocrate's country retreat.

PRONUNCIATION GUIDE

In French these names are accented on the final syllable.

Léonide	LAY-OH-<u>NEED</u>
Phocion	FOH-SEE-<u>AW(N)</u>
Aspasie	AH-SPAH-<u>ZEE</u>
Corine	KOH-<u>REEN</u>
Hermidas	AIR-MEE-<u>DAHS</u>(hard s)
Dimas	DEE-<u>MAHS</u>(hard s)
Agis	AH-<u>ZHEES</u>(hard s)
Léontine	LAY-AW(N)-<u>TEEN</u>
Hermocrate	AIR-MOH-<u>KRAHT</u>

Harlequin, a recognizable word in English, needn't perhaps be pronounced in the French manner. However, in French he is

Arlequin	AR-LE-<u>KA(N)</u>

NOTE

The Triumph of Love, a comedy in three acts and in prose, was played for the first time by the Comédie Italienne in Paris on March 12, 1732. The Comédie Italienne, a troupe of Italian *commedia dell' arte* actors, had initially played to the Parisians in Italian but eventually learned to play in the host tongue. Marivaux (1688-1763) wrote a number of plays for them, and the characters in many of those plays are named for the actors' regular *commedia* characters. It is Harlequin who bears the *commedia* standard in *The Triumph of Love*.

As I could not imagine a performance of *The Triumph of Love* in which Harlequin, mercurial wag and improviser, would not lapse from Marivaux's script into improvisation, I have provided an intermezzo at the beginning of Act II, which is an adaptation of an old *commedia* scenario entitled "Harlequin In Love." I developed this scene in rehearsal with John Michael Higgins, the inspired Harlequin of the first performance of this adaptation.

Marivaux honored different theatrical traditions in his distinctive, curiously moving blend of comedy and drama. The characters in *The Triumph of Love* are the recognizable grandchildren of Racine's noble, eloquent, long-suffering characters, but they are also clearly descended from the mischievous, volatile, lusty *commedia* family. And they share the stage with Harlequin himself—the original presumptuous, enigmatic, highly histrionic, irresistible witty-idiot *commedia* clown. The juxtaposition onstage of this unabashed buffoon and men and women in complex, serious situations should provoke wonderment and delight. This is an essence of Marivaux.

Marivaux's plays are about what happens to people who are falling in love, which has earned the playwright a reputation for frivolity. But when you hear the heartbeats of his characters, you realize that they are going through hell. Love, Marivaux seems to say, gets you in touch with *everything*—not just the good things, but also the nervousness, the dread, the anxiety, the jealousy; love is the key to the world of emotion, to self-knowledge and to freedom. Love is costly, dangerous even. This is another essence of Marivaux.

So Marivaux's plays are really about the agony of change—the aspirations, the self-question, the doubt, the yearning, the fear, the excitement, the not knowing. Marivaux, who dined and argued with leading thinkers of the Enlightenment (including Diderot, Voltaire and Rousseau), caught the spirit of that time, profound internal change, in the trap of love. In Marivaux's characters— struggling to understand what is happening to them and to accept the sobering notion of change at great cost to themselves—we can see the image of Enlightenment Europe.

S.W.

THE TRIUMPH OF LOVE

ACT I

Scene 1

Enter LÉONIDE and CORINE.

LÉONIDE. These are the gardens of the philosopher, Hermocrate. I think.

CORINE. But madam, won't we be thought rude for having entered unannounced? We don't know a soul here.

LÉONIDE. No, the gate was open, and furthermore we have come to speak to the master of the house.

(THEY look around.)

LÉONIDE. Let's stay here a moment. It's time for you to know more.

CORINE. Finally! I've been dying of curiosity. But Princess Léonide, would you be so kind as to let me ask the questions?

LÉONIDE. As you wish.

CORINE. First you leave the court and the city, and you come here practically unattended to one of your country homes, where you require that I follow you ...

LÉONIDE. Exactly.

CORINE. Now, I have learned to paint—and you know that—and soon after we arrive in the country you knock on

11

my door, lock yourself in my room, and show me two portraits, which you ask me to reproduce in miniature— one is of a man of fifty, the other of a woman of shall we say forty, and both are reasonably handsome.

LÉONIDE.   That is true—

CORINE. Let me speak. Once the copies are finished you start a rumor that you are feeling unwell and do not wish to be seen. You dress me up as a man, I dress *you* up as man, and then we set out together in this ... get-up— incognito, you with the name of Phocion and I with that of Hermidas. And after a fifteen-minute walk here we are in the gardens of Hermocrate—a philosopher in whose philosophy I believe you have little interest.

LÉONIDE. More interest than you may think.

CORINE. So what does it all mean—the copied portraits, the feigned indisposition, the seclusion in the country, the change of sexes? Who are this man and this woman I painted? Why a philosopher's garden? What do you have in store for him? What do you have in store for *me*!? Where are we headed, and how will it come out? (*A beat.*) These are some of my questions.

LÉONIDE. Listen. Let's start at the beginning. You know that, in a sense, I am not the true princess. My uncle, who was a great general, usurped the throne. King Cleomones had stolen away from him the woman he loved, so my uncle locked them both up and seized the kingdom. The old king died eventually in the dungeon. But what you don't know, Corine, is that that woman died in childbirth, producing a *prince*! Who mysteriously disappeared without a trace. My uncle had no children, so my father succeeded him, and I succeeded my father.

CORINE. Yes, but you haven't yet said one thing about our disguise or the portraits I painted, and that's all I want to know

LÉONIDE. Be patient. Now, that *prince*! That prince, born in prison and taken away at birth by an unknown hand—that prince is the true heir to the throne I sit on. And I have just found out where he is.

CORINE. Well thank heavens for that. And will you soon have him in your power?

LÉONIDE. On the contrary, he will have me in his.

CORINE. You, Princess? *No one* will have power over you! The throne is yours—I won't let him take it from you.

LÉONIDE. Ssshhhhh! Some years after disappearing from the prison, this prince was handed over by a relative of the king to the wise Hermocrate and his spinster sister, who for the last ten years have raised him, in secret and very strictly, as my enemy. I heard this whole tale from a servant who worked until recently on this very estate.

CORINE. Servants can lie; we need better sources.

LÉONIDE. But I am not here to disprove the story.

A sense of ... what is right ... of fairness ... and some other sense ... I'm not sure what ... brings me here. First of all I wanted to see Agis (that's the prince's name). The servant promised to point him out to me. He said that Agis and Hermocrate take a daily walk in the wood near my chateau. So I left the city as you know, I came here, I dismissed my escort ... entered that wood ... and saw Agis. He was sitting under a tree, reading a book.

Before that moment I had often heard talk of love, but I knew it only as a word.

Imagine, Corine, if the Graces endowed one man with all their gifts—nobility, elegance, charm and beauty, and you can barely begin to imagine the charms of the face, and of the form ... of Agis.

CORINE. What I am beginning to imagine very clearly is that the figure he cuts may explain the figures we're cutting, out here in the pastures.

LÉONIDE. I forgot to tell you that as I withdrew Hermocrate appeared and stopped me! He asked me whether the princess—meaning *me*!—ever walked in these woods. I was startled by his question, but I realized that he did not know me by sight, and I told him that I had heard she was about. And then I went back to the chateau.

CORINE. Well now this, madam, is quite an unusual tale.

LÉONIDE. The goal I have set for myself is even more unusual. And I feigned illness, and secluded and disguised myself, so that I would be free to pursue it.

I'll introduce myself to Hermocrate as Phocion, a young traveler drawn here by the reputation of his wisdom. I will ask him to let me spend time with him, to learn at his knee. I will meanwhile make every effort to speak with Agis and prepare him to feel differently about me. I am born to blood he has been taught to hate, so I dare not tell him my name.

Now, love, make some use of those charms for which I am so often complimented, and protect me from the hate I know he feels for me.

CORINE. But madam, if Hermocrate were to recognize, under your disguise, the woman he spoke to in the wood, you'd never set foot in his house.

LÉONIDE. I have thought of that, Corine. If he recognizes me, so much the worse for him, because I have set him a snare from which all his rational thinking could not possibly protect him. Mind you, I will not be happy if he forces me to use it, because my *goal* is honorable, even if the snare is ... well ... less so. I am in love. And there is justice to be done.

I need two or three encounters with Agis; I don't expect more than a few, but they are essential, and if I can have them only at Hermocrate's expense, well, then, so be it.

CORINE. But isn't the spinster sister also liable to be inflexible—even with a stranger as young and handsome as yourself?

LÉONIDE. If she stands in my way, so much the worse for *her*. I would no sooner spare her than I would her brother.

CORINE. But madam, if I understand what you're saying, you would have to deceive them both. This duplicity ... doesn't it go against the grain?

LÉONIDE. Despite the worthy purposes that prompt it, yes. I find it distasteful. I would be loath to resort to it. But it will get me even with Hermocrate and his sister, who deserve it.

Since Agis has been with them they have done all they can to inspire him to hate me. They paint the most odious portrait of me, and all without knowing me, without knowing my nature, or any of the virtues with which heaven might have blessed it. They have stirred up all my enemies, and they continue to raise new ones against me. Why do they want to hurt me? Is it because I usurped a throne? But I'm not the one who usurped it! Besides, how could I have returned it when its legitimate heir has never come forward and is thought to have died?

No, Corine, I needn't be worried by scruples where they are concerned.

CORINE. Are the portraits of them?

LÉONIDE. Yes. The portraits .... I may use them, I may not. Guard them well, and play along, Corine, whatever happens. And I'll keep you apprised of things as we go.

(HARLEQUIN enters unseen.)

Scene 2

HARLEQUIN. (*Aside.*) Now who have we here?

CORINE. This will all have to be quite a performance, madam, considering your sex.

HARLEQUIN. (*Surprising them.*). Yes indeed, *madam!* Considering your *sex!* Speak up, men! Are you women!?

LÉONIDE. God in Heaven, I'm done for.

(The WOMEN start to leave.)

HARLEQUIN. Uh uh uh, my beauties! Before you go, please—we ought to settle this together. At first I took you for two fellows on the loose, but I must apologize, for now I see you are just two loose women!

LÉONIDE. All is lost, Corine.

CORINE. (*To Léonide, aside.*) No, madam, let me take care of this, and don't give it a thought. He doesn't fool me for a minute—look at his face. He can be ... handled.

HARLEQUIN. And he is, moreover, an honest man who has never let smuggled goods get by him! (*Grabbing the tails of their coats.*) I therefore seize this merchandise. I shall have them close the gates!

CORINE. And I shall certainly stop you from doing that, because you would very much regret it.

HARLEQUIN. Prove that I'd regret it, and I'll let you go.

LÉONIDE. (*Offering him several gold coins.*) Is this proof enough?

(*HARLEQUIN takes them.*)

LÉONIDE. Now wouldn't it have been foolish to pass that up?

HARLEQUIN. Yes ... well ... so it would seem, because I feel very good about having it.

CORINE. Do you still feel like making a stink?

HARLEQUIN. I am *beginning* to not feel like it.

CORINE. More proof, madam.

LÉONIDE. (*Giving him more.*) Here, take this too. Happier?

HARLEQUIN. (*Pointing at the gold in his hand.*) That is the *exact* extent of my stubbornness! But munificent ladies! What are you doing?

CORINE. Oh it's nothing. My lady saw Agis in the forest, and she lost her heart to him.

HARLEQUIN. Well *that's* honest, anyway.

CORINE. Now madam, who is independent ... and rich ... and who would readily marry him, would like a chance to attract his interest.

HARLEQUIN. That's even more honest ...

CORINE. But madam could not do this without engaging him in conversation, without perhaps even living in the same house for a while.

HARLEQUIN. To enjoy all of its ... conveniences ...

CORINE. And this would not be possible if she presented herself dressed as the woman she is, because Hermocrate would not allow it, and Agis himself would shun her, because of what he's been taught by the great philosopher.

HARLEQUIN. God forbid there should be love in that house! The philosophy of Hermocrate is about as hostile to love as any philosophy could be—and Agis and Léontine are faithful followers. You know, I'm the only one around here with any know-how in affairs of the heart.

LÉONIDE. We saw that immediately.

CORINE. So all this is why madam decided to come in disguise, and you can see there's nothing wrong in it.

HARLEQUIN. By God, nothing could be more reasonable. My lady happened to take a fancy to Agis, so what of it? We all take what we can get; that only makes sense. Onward, obliging gentlemen! Good luck to you. I am at your service. (*To Léonide.*) You have lost your heart, concentrate on finding someone else's .... (*To Corine.*) I'd happily lose *mine* ... if someone would care to find it.

LÉONIDE. Well in this matter *my* loss will be your gain. You are a lucky man.

CORINE. Don't forget that madam is called Phocion, and I am Hermidas.

LÉONIDE. And above all—Agis must never know who we are.

HARLEQUIN. Fear not, Lord Phocion. (*To Corine.*) Don't worry, chum. See, I know how to handle myself.

CORINE. Quiet, someone's coming ...

(DIMAS enters.)

Scene 3

DIMAS. And just who are *you* talking to, friend?

HARLEQUIN. I am talking to people.

DIMAS. For God's sake, I can see that. But what people? And who do they want?

LÉONIDE. Lord Hermocrate.

DIMAS. Well this isn't the way in. The master told me not to let any ... antelopers wander around in his garden, so you better go back the way you came and knock at the front gate.

LÉONIDE. We found the garden doors open. Aren't strangers allowed to make mistakes?

DIMAS. No! And they're not allowed to sneak around either, and don't give me this about slipping through open drawers. You have the decency to call out to the gardener, you ask for his permission, you show him certain ... considerations, he grants you his permission, and *then* the drawers are slipped open!

HARLEQUIN. Easy does it, friend, you are speaking to a very important person.

DIMAS. Easy to see that the person is rich, since this person has a lot to guard, and I guard only my garden. But this person should take another road.

(AGIS enters.)

Scene 4

AGIS. What on earth is all this noise about? Dimas, at whom are you shouting?

DIMAS. At this pretty young thing that jumps over the wall to pick the fruit off our trees.

LÉONIDE. You arrive just in time, sir, to rid me of this man. I came to pay my respects to Lord Hermocrate, I found the garden open, and he wants me out.

AGIS. Enough Dimas, you've made a mistake. Run off and tell Léontine a worthy stranger wishes to speak to Hermocrate.

(DIMAS leaves.)

AGIS. I must apologize, sir, for the rustic greeting he gave you; Hermocrate himself will apologize. Your appearance alone suggests that you be shown every consideration.

HARLEQUIN. For that matter, *both* of them have pretty faces.

LÉONIDE. The gardener was indeed brusque, but your compliments redress the wrong. And if as you say my appearance inspires you to ... consider me ... favorably, why that would be one of the kindest services it could do me. But mine is only *one* of the fortuitous appearances in this garden today.

AGIS. (*A bit abashed.*) Well let's not make too much of it, sir, but your appearance does do you credit. And though we met but a moment ago, I assure you that one could not be more ... favorably inclined ... towards someone than I am towards you.

HARLEQUIN. That makes four of us.

CORINE. (*To Harlequin.*) Let's take a walk and discuss these *inclinations*.

(*CORINE leads HARLEQUIN off. LÉONIDE and AGIS are left facing each other.*)

AGIS. May I ask who it is, for whom I feel such ... affection?

LÉONIDE. Someone who feels it in return, and would ... forever.

AGIS. Tell me more; I sense I've made a friend I might soon lose.

LÉONIDE. Our separation would never be *my* doing, sir.

(*A beat.*)

AGIS. (*Changing tack.*) What do you want from Hermocrate? Do you want to study with him? He has educated me, you know, and I am proud to say he loves me.

LÉONIDE. His reputation drew me here. I intended only to spend some time at his side, but since meeting you that intention has given way to another, more pressing one, which is ... to see you for as long as I possibly can.

AGIS. And then what?

LÉONIDE. I don't know. (*A beat.*) You will decide that. I'll take only your advice in this matter.

AGIS. Then I advise you never to lose sight of me.

LÉONIDE. Then we will always be together.

AGIS. I would like that. (*A beat.*) With all my heart. But look—here comes Léontine.

HARLEQUIN. (*Returning with CORINE.*) The mistress approaches. I don't like that pious look of hers at all.

(*DIMAS returns with LÉONTINE.*)

Scene 5

DIMAS. (*Presenting Léonide and Corine.*) Look madam, here is the squire I told you about. And this pest is in his ... retina.

LÉONTINE. (*To Léonide.*) I was told, sir, that you wish to speak to my brother, but he's not here just now. While we await his return, might you confide in me what it is you want with him?

LÉONIDE. I have no secret business with him, madam. I have come to ask him a favor, but perhaps you will grant it in his stead.

LÉONTINE. Explain yourself.

LÉONIDE. My name is Phocion, madam, a name that might be known to you. Perhaps you have heard of my father ...

LÉONTINE. (*Interrupting.*) Of course.

LÉONIDE. I have been traveling for some time, alone, and with only my wits to rely on—to educate my heart and my mind.

DIMAS. And to pick the fruit off our trees.

LÉONTINE. Leave us, Dimas.

LÉONIDE. I have met many scholars whose virtue and learning set them apart from other men. Some even allowed me to stay with them and study for a while; and I was hoping that the august Hermocrate would not refuse me, for a few days ... the same privilege.

LÉONTINE. By your appearance, sir, you seem to be entirely worthy of the hospitality you have found elsewhere; but it will not be possible for Hermocrate to offer it to you here. Important reasons, which Agis knows well, make that impossible. I am terribly sorry that your appeal must be denied.

AGIS. We're not lacking in *beds*.

HARLEQUIN. One of them could certainly stay in *my* room!

LÉONTINE. No, but you know better than anyone, Agis, that this cannot be—that we have made ourselves a rule not to share our retreat with anyone.

AGIS. But I have promised Lord Phocion to urge you to consider an exception, for a virtuous person, a friend— surely that would not violate the rule.

LÉONTINE. I could never change my feelings.

HARLEQUIN. (*Aside.*) Pig-headed cow!

LÉONIDE. But madam, can you be impervious to such good intentions?

LÉONTINE. In spite of myself, yes, I must be.

AGIS. Hermocrate will persuade you, madam.

LÉONTINE. I am sure he will think as I do.

LÉONIDE. (*Aside.*) The time has come .... (*Aloud.*) I will not press you further, madam, but may I make so bold as to ask for a moment alone with you?

LÉONTINE. Frankly, sir, your tenacity is off-putting, and will not help your cause, but if you insist ...

LÉONIDE. (*To Agis.*) Will you leave us for a moment?

(AGIS leaves. Exeunt HARLEQUIN and CORINE.)

Scene 6

LÉONIDE. (*Aside, as HARLEQUIN and CORINE leave.*) May love bless this lie. (*Aloud, at first hesitant, as SHE tests the waters.*) Since you cannot grant what I ask, madam, it would be unthinkable to press you further, but will you consider doing me another kindness—that is ... to advise me in a matter that will ... entirely determine my peace of mind ... for the rest of my life?

LÉONTINE. I would advise you to wait for Hermocrate, sir; better to consult him than me.

LÉONIDE. No, madam, in this ... matter, you can help me far more than he can. For I need someone who is not severe ... but rather ... well, forbearing; whose judgment is ... tempered ... by compassion. I have found that sweet mixture more often in your sex than in ours. Listen to me, please, madam. I appeal to all that is good in you.

LÉONTINE. I am not sure exactly what you're getting at, but a stranger deserves certain considerations; so speak. I am listening.

LÉONIDE. A few days ago, as I was passing through these parts, I saw a woman ... who did not see me. I will describe her to you; perhaps you know her.

(A beat. SHE begins her love-making cautiously.)

LÉONIDE. She is tall ... but not too tall, yet ... still she is ... really quite ... majestic. I have never seen such nobility of bearing. I have never seen a union of such tender features with an air so imposing, so controlled ... so stern, even. One could not help loving her ... but with a love that is timid ... even frightened, of the awe she inspires .... (*Gaining confidence.*) She is *young* ... but not with that youthful flightiness that I have always deplored— all unfulfilled promise, knowing how to amuse the eye but not yet deserving to touch the heart. No, she is young in a different way—at an age when her charms, at the height of their powers, are richly and eloquently blended, when she can take pleasure in knowing exactly who she is, when her well-tempered soul has lit up her beauty with its unmistakable, subtle radiance.

LÉONTINE. (*Ill at ease.*) I do not know her, sir; this woman is unknown to me; and the picture you paint of her is surely too flattering.

LÉONIDE. This woman, whom I adore, madam, is so many times more wonderful than the picture I have painted of her. I tell you, I had no intention of stopping here, but I was transfixed by her beauty, and I watched her ... closely ... for a long time. She was conversing with someone; she smiled from time to time; and I saw in her gestures a certain sweetness, a generosity ... a *kindness*. And I also saw it shining, with piercing clarity, from her solemn, quiet eyes.

LÉONTINE. (*Aside.*) Who can he be speaking of?

LÉONIDE. After a while she left. When I asked who she was I learned that she is the sister of a distinguished and respectable man.

LÉONTINE. (*Aside.*) Am I dreaming?

LÉONIDE. She has never married, but lives with her brother in a retreat whose stoical pleasures she prefers to the confusion of a world inhospitable to the truly virtuous. In short, I heard only good things about her, and so my reason, as much as my heart, finally determined that I must love her.

LÉONTINE. (*Moved.*) Spare me the rest, sir. I do not know what love is, and I would advise you poorly on something of which I have no understanding.

LÉONIDE. Please, let me finish—and don't let this word Love shock you; the love I am speaking of is not at all profane, it is pure, ennobling, virtuous. In fact my love of virtue *kindles* my love for this woman; these two loves are inextricably mingled—they are the same love. For if I love *her*, if I see her form as something perfectly beautiful, it is because my soul sees in everything, everywhere, the image of her perfectly virtuous heart.

LÉONTINE. Please let me go, sir. I am expected at the house, and we have been speaking a long time.

LÉONIDE. I'm nearly through, madam. Transported and changed forever by these feelings, I vowed to love her forever, and in so doing to consecrate my days to the service of virtue itself. I resolved to speak to her brother and, under the pretext of improving myself, to get his permission to stay in his house. And once there, close to her—submissive ... attentive ... tender ... I would make her a gift of my love, my respect, my reverence, and my passion, for the Gods have willed it so.

LÉONTINE. (*Aside.*) I am trapped. Can I free myself?

LÉONIDE. I did as I had resolved. I came here to speak to her brother but found her instead. I implored her, in vain, to grant my request, but she denied me, and drove me to my present state. Imagine, madam, my heart—trembling and confused before her .... Surely she might see its gentleness, its pain; surely she might feel some pity, if nothing more than that.

But she has refused me even pity, so I have come to *you*, madam, despondent, and here at your feet I confide in you all my sorrow. (*SHE falls to her knees.*)

LÉONTINE. What are you doing, sir?

LÉONIDE. I desperately need your help and advice with her.

LÉONTINE. After what I have just heard, I myself need advice from the gods.

LÉONIDE. But your heart, madam, is blessed with the wisdom of the gods—*follow your heart!*

LÉONTINE. My heart?! But the heart is an enemy to peace, to serenity ...

LÉONIDE. Would you be less peaceful or serene for having been generous?

LÉONTINE. Ah Phocion, you say you love virtue; can you love it if you corrupt it?

LÉONIDE. To love—is it to corrupt?

LÉONTINE. But what is your *purpose*?

LÉONIDE. I have given you my life. I want it to be yours. Will you suffer my presence here for just a few days? For now that is my only wish, and if you grant it, I know that Hermocrate will allow it.

LÉONTINE. But *you're* the one who'll suffer—*you*, who love me.

LÉONIDE. What good is love that does not cost?

LÉONTINE. But can a virtuous love inspire feelings that are not virtuous? I don't understand! What have you come here to do, Phocion? What is happening to me? It is inconceivable! Would you have me lose my heart? Would you have me lose my *reason*? Must I now give my life over to my feelings? Am I to love you—I who have never loved? When in the end your flattery is meaningless, for you are young, you are handsome ... while I am neither.

LÉONIDE. But how can you say that?

LÉONTINE. Very well sir, I admit that I had my small share of beauty—or so it was said. Nature did endow me with certain charms, but I have always held them in contempt. Perhaps you will make me come to regret that I disdained them. It shames me to say it, but they are gone .... Or what little is left of them soon will be.

LÉONIDE. What good does it do you to say this, Léontine? You can't convince me that I do not see what I see. Perhaps you hope to sway me with these very charms you speak of .... Ah, could you *ever* have been more enchanting?!

LÉONTINE. I am no longer what I was.

LÉONIDE. Let us not argue, madam. Yes, I concede it—enchanting as you are, your youth will soon pass, and I am still young; but souls have no age.

So I ask you again to let me stay. And I am going to ask Hermocrate, too. I will die of grief if the two of you cannot find it in your hearts to indulge me.

LÉONTINE. I don't know ... what I should do ... yet. Hermocrate is coming. I will speak on your behalf, until I can decide.

(AGIS returns with HERMOCRATE, HARLEQUIN reappears.)

Scene 7

HERMOCRATE. *(To Agis.)* Is this the young man of whom you spoke?

AGIS. Yes sir, the very one.

HARLEQUIN. It is I who had the honor of speaking to him first, sir, and I took *very* good care of him while we waited for you.

LÉONTINE. This, Hermocrate, is the son of Phocion. His esteem for you brought him here to us. He is a student of reason, and is traveling to improve his mind. Several of your peers welcomed him in their houses. He hopes for the same welcome from you and asks for it with an ardor that commands attention. I promised to intercede for him. Now I leave you together.

(LEONTINE sighs audibly as SHE leaves.)

AGIS. And if my vote counts, I add it to Léontine's, sir.

(AGIS exits.)

HARLEQUIN. And I add mine into the bargain.

HERMOCRATE. (*Recognizing Léonide.*) But you ...

LÉONIDE. I am very grateful for their kind words on my behalf, sir. I am even more grateful that you might recognize ... in me ... a worthy follower.

HERMOCRATE. And I thank you, sir, for your kind words. But someone who follows as well as you ... does not seem to need *me* ... to lead him. Perhaps it would be wise to ask you a few questions in private. (*To Harlequin.*) Go.

(HARLEQUIN departs.)

Scene 8

HERMOCRATE. Either I am mistaken, sir, or you are not unknown to me.

LÉONIDE. I, sir?

HERMOCRATE. I have my reasons for wanting to speak to you in private; I thought I could spare you some embarrassment. I don't need lightning to confirm my suspicions.

LÉONIDE. And what suspicions are those?

HERMOCRATE. Your name is not Phocion at all.

LÉONIDE. (*Aside.*) He remembers our meeting.

HERMOCRATE. The boy whose name you have borrowed is in Athens at present; I happen to know this from his tutor.

LÉONIDE. There must be someone else with the same name.

HERMOCRATE. And that's not all; this assumed name is not your only disguise. Admit it, madam, I have seen you before, walking in the wood.

LÉONIDE. (*Pretending to be surprised.*) You speak the truth, sir.

HERMOCRATE. So you see all of your character witnesses here did you no good. At least they won't have to see you blush.

LÉONIDE. If I *blush* it does me no good, sir—it's a reflex I regret, and it has misled you. My disguise does not conceal anything of which I should be ashamed.

HERMOCRATE. I am beginning to see your design, and I see nothing in it at all becoming to the innocent virtues of your sex—and certainly nothing of which you should be *proud*. The idea of coming here to take away my student, Agis, of working your dangerous feminine charms on him, of stirring up in his heart a turmoil that is almost always disastrous—this idea, it seems to me, would naturally make you blush.

LÉONIDE. Agis? Who, that young man who was just here? Are *those* your suspicions? What do you see in me to justify them? Or do you suspect me simply because I am a woman? Ah, that it should be you who does me this injury! And that intentions such as mine should inspire it!

No, sir, I have not come here to stir up Agis' heart—far from it. He was raised by your hand, and he is strong through the wisdom of your teaching, but to assume this disguise for *his* sake would not have been necessary. If I loved him, I would hope to conquer him with less effort—I would let him see me as I am; I would let my eyes speak. His inexperience and my "dangerous feminine charms" would have given me the edge. But it is not to his heart that mine inclines. The heart I seek is a more difficult one to entrap—oblivious to the power in my eyes, indifferent to beauty. And as I cannot resort to my feminine charms, I have made a point of not putting them on display. I have hidden them under this disguise because they are useless to me.

HERMOCRATE. But why do you want to stay in my house, madam, if your scheme has nothing to do with Agis?

LÉONIDE. Why is it always Agis?! (*A beat.*) Don't hold my appearance against me—my "scheme" might be not only innocent, but actually honorable. You will see, I shall stick to it with a determination that will dissolve your suspicions, and when you know its purpose I daresay you may even respect me for it.

Don't talk to me any more about Agis, I am not thinking of him at all.

Do you want irrefutable proof? *That* would hardly be "becoming to the innocent virtues of my sex." I do not come here with a woman's cunning, or vanity, or pride. I come with something finer and stronger.

We were speaking of your suspicions; a few words might dispel them .... Will the one I love agree to give me his hand? (*A beat. Extending her hand.*) Here is mine.

And Agis is not here to accept my offer.

HERMOCRATE. (*Embarrassed.*) I no longer know to whom this is addressed.

LÉONIDE. You do know, sir, for I have just told you. I could not have said it more clearly by saying your name. Hermocrate.

HERMOCRATE. I, madam!

LÉONIDE. You are enlightened, my lord.

HERMOCRATE. (*Disconcerted.*) I am, I suppose, though your words trouble me deeply. That a heart such as yours could be moved by me ...

LÉONIDE. Listen to me, my lord. I must explain myself after burdening you with this.

HERMOCRATE. No, madam, I'll hear no more. You needn't justify what you have said to me, I won't judge you for it, but for goodness' sake leave me alone. Was I made to be loved? No. You lay siege to a solitary heart, to which love must remain a stranger. My severity, my self-denial, must combat your youth and your beauty.

LÉONIDE. But I am not asking you to share my feelings. I have no hope of that—or if I do, I disavow it. But allow me to finish. I have told you that I love you; now I must explain myself.

HERMOCRATE. But reason cautions me against hearing any more.

LÉONIDE. But my virtue, and my honor, which I have just compromised, demand that I continue. Please, my lord, I aspire only to be worthy in your eyes, my heart desires only that reward. Why should you not hear me out? What have you to fear from me—a handful of charms rendered ineffectual by my confession? And a frailty that you disdain and that is powerless in combat against you?

HERMOCRATE. I wish I were not even aware of that frailty.

LÉONIDE. Yes, my lord, I love you, but do not mistake my love for something it is not. This is no rash infatuation, and my confession is not irrational, nor has it slipped from me in an emotional moment. I am in full possession of my faculties. I don't owe my confession to love—love could never have gotten it out of me—but to ... a sense of what is right.

I am telling you that I love you so that I will feel confusion—mortification, chagrin. Faced with the grim prospect of feeling such things, maybe I could be cured of my love for you! If I could feel shame at my weakness, I might conquer it; if I could regain my honor, I could use it to fight you off.

I am telling you that I love you not so that you should love *me*, but so that you should teach me how *not* to love *you*. You hate love, you reject it. I am all for that, but help me to reject love as you do! Teach me how to get my heart back from you, protect me from my attraction to you. I am not asking to be loved, I swear it, but I *desire* to be loved. Extinguish this desire! I beg you, save me from yourself!

HERMOCRATE. Madam, I can help you in this way only: I absolutely do not wish to love you; let my indifference be your cure, and put an end to this scene. Your words are poison.

LÉONIDE. Great Gods, I expected your indifference, but do you deny me utterly? I have poured out my heart, I have been as brave as I know how to be, I have denied *myself*— and this is your response? Does the wise man serve only himself?

HERMOCRATE. I am not at all wise, madam.

LÉONIDE. You may be right, but I need time to discover your faults for myself. *Please* .... My name is Aspasie, and like you I have lived in seclusion, mistress of myself, and of a sizeable fortune, ignorant of love and contemptuous of any effort to arouse it in me.

HERMOCRATE. (*Aside.*) Why am I standing here?

LÉONIDE. Then I met you, walking alone as I have so often. I did not know who you were, but looking at you, I was moved. It seems my heart found you out, Hermocrate.

HERMOCRATE. No! Stop! I cannot endure any more of this. If as you say you are motivated by a sense of what is right, Aspasie, we must end this conversation.

LÉONIDE. I suppose all this must seem frivolous, but I assure you, the importance of recovering my reason is not.

HERMOCRATE. And the importance of safeguarding my own is becoming more and more urgent. As unversed in love as I may be, I have eyes: you have charms .... And you love me.

LÉONIDE. I have charms, you say. What, my lord, you can see them? (*A beat.*) Do you fear them?

HERMOCRATE. Fear is an emotion I avoid.

LÉONIDE. But your avoidance of it proves that you *are* afraid! You do not love me yet, but you are afraid you might. I can't help hoping that it will be so.

HERMOCRATE. You confuse me; I'm not answering you well; I will say no more.

LÉONIDE. Well, my lord, let us go then. Let us walk. Let us find Léontine. (*Turning back to him.*) Let me stay on here a while. And when you are ready, you can give me your decision.

HERMOCRATE. Go, Aspasie. I will follow ....

(*Exit LÉONIDE.*)

Scene 9

HERMOCRATE. I almost lost my way there. (*A beat.*)
What should I decide?

(*DIMAS is passing.*)

HERMOCRATE. Dimas, come here. Do you see that
young man who just left me? I want you to keep your eye
on him, follow him as closely as you can, and see if he
tries to engage Agis in conversation. Do you hear? I have
always appreciated your loyalty, and you could find no
better way to show it than by doing exactly as I have told
you.
DIMAS. In two shakes of a lamb's tail.
HERMOCRATE. I want to know what he is thinking.
DIMAS. I will bring you his brain in a basket.

BLACKOUT

INTERMEZZO

(HARLEQUIN is discovered in a pose of despair, crying noisily. HE plays the scene with many changes of voice, gesturing wildly and moving suddenly from one part of the stage to another.)

HARLEQUIN. Ah, unhappy me! Will I ever be able to marry Corine? The situation is rich with misery. First of all, does she even love me? I would think that ... to look at me is to love me, and when she *is* looking at me I am sure that she does love me; it's only when she stops looking at me that I'm not sure she does any more, or ever did really. And even if she did, or does, or always will, she can't just *have* me, as she is a lady's maid, a servant, one of her mistress's belongings, who has many rights as her petticoat. But I err! For her petticoat can do precisely what she cannot: rise! *(HE laughs.)* And though I am but a servant and have no rights, I have only to think of her, and I can do what she cannot: rise! *(More laughter.)* And I cannot just have *her*, either, because not only do I *serve*, but I serve Hermocrate, and the chances of his allowing me to leave his service to pursue *love* ... are slimmer with every panting breast ... uh, *passing breath*! Ah, how shall I be able to live without Corine? I would rather die first. *(A beat.) Die*?! Die. That's it. Let me see ... some unusual sort of death. An heroic death, an *horrible* death ... an *hanging* death! *That's* it! *(Racing frantically about, miming the actions HE describes.)* I shall go to my room,

tie a chair to a crossbeam, climb upon a rope, place the
chair around my neck, kick away the room, and .... No. I
shall go to my room, tie a rope to a crossbeam, kick away
the chair ... *(Cheerfully:)* and I'm hanged! I'll hang now,
then elope, and then when I'm arrested for the crime of
escaping my master I'll not have to hang again, because
who would hang a man who's already been hanged?! It's
perfect!

*(HE notices that HE's hanged himself and responds with
     frantic jerks and terrible noises of death. Eventually HE
     manages to cut himself down, landing with a thud.)*

HARLEQUIN. Ha, idiotic servant fool! Poor passionate
put-upon Corine! Ah, blasted mistress Phocion, why have
you come here?!

(HE muses, pensive and still.)

HARLEQUIN. Perhaps if I were just to be hilarious for
a while I could amuse myself to death.

ACT II

Scene 1

DIMAS enters.

DIMAS. For God's sake get over here. I tell you, ever since these poachers got here, its impossible to get a word with you. You're always off in some corner whispering with that whippersnapper valet.

HARLEQUIN. My very old friend, I'm just being civil. If I don't pay constant attention to you, it doesn't mean I love you any less.

DIMAS. But being civil doesn't mean hiding things from very old friends. You know, friendship is like wine, by God—the older the better. That's how it is.

HARLEQUIN. What a tasteful observation. We'll drink to that whenever you say, and it will be my treat.

DIMAS. Aren't you lordly! You say that as if it rained wine *and* money. Think you could scare up enough of either to make it worth my while?

HARLEQUIN. Don't you worry about a thing.

DIMAS. Bless my heart but you're quite the magpie. But then, I'm a magpie too.

HARLEQUIN. (*Suspicious.*) And since when are we scavenger birds?

DIMAS. Ha ha, don't think I don't know you've already picked our visitors clean. You see, I saw you counting your stash.

39

HARLEQUIN. Ah! It's truly a day of reckoning!

DIMAS. *(Aside.)* I think I've got him. *(Aloud.)* Listen friend, the master is very upset—he doesn't know what to make of it all.

HARLEQUIN. I suppose he also saw me counting my stash?

DIMAS. Oh it's much worse than that. *(Continuing with utmost confidentiality.)* He thinks there's something going on around here. He wants me to play the fox and sniff it out. He wants me to plow those two tresspastures and ... gather in their harvest. He wants to know why they cropped up, and what's growing in them. Understand?

HARLEQUIN. Not exactly. Is this how foxes talk?

DIMAS. Uh uh uh! You won't get anything out of me! I only want to find out what *you* know. To begin at the beginning, you're not supposed to tell the master who these vagabonds really are, right?

HARLEQUIN. He'll never get it out of *me*!

DIMAS. Well *you* don't have to *tell* him! He only listens to me anyway, because I see everything.

HARLEQUIN. So you know who they are then?

DIMAS. For God's sake! I know them root and branch.

HARLEQUIN. Oh, I thought I was the only one who knew about them.

DIMAS. You? Ha! Maybe you don't know the first *thing* about them.

HARLEQUIN. Oh but I do.

DIMAS. I bet you don't, I don't think so. You could never figure it out.

HARLEQUIN. I could too! And anyway, they told me themselves!

DIMAS. What?

HARLEQUIN. That they're women!
DIMAS. (*Astounded.*) They're *women*!!!

(A beat.)

HARLEQUIN. What? You mean you didn't know? You *sneak*!
DIMAS. No I didn't, but by God I do now! I'm a fox.
HARLEQUIN. You're a *fiend*!
DIMAS. I'm a fiend!
HARLEQUIN. And I'm a fool.
DIMAS. I'm going to make the most of this! I'll tell everyone! What a tale! They're *women*!
HARLEQUIN. Dimas, you have cut my throat.
DIMAS. What do I care about *your* throat? Ha! Women in *my* garden, making payments to the valet behind *my* back! Let the blood flow! They are *dresspassers*! And they must be called to accounts!
HARLEQUIN. So, my friend, you want money, do you?
DIMAS. I would be a damned fool if I didn't. And I bet I can guess where it's going to come from.
HARLEQUIN. I will prevail upon the lady to buy back my blunder, I promise you.
DIMAS. This blunder will not be cheap, I can tell you.
HARLEQUIN. I realize it's going to be overpriced.
DIMAS. And payments begin now: first you tell me every little thing about this swindle. Like how much money did she give you? How many gold pieces? How much loose change? How big is her budgy? Tell the truth.
HARLEQUIN. She gave me twenty gold pieces.

DIMAS. Twenty gold pieces?! That's a new *life*! You could buy a small farm for that. (*A beat.*) What does she want here?

HARLEQUIN. Well, Agis stole her heart while she was out on a walk. And she got herself up like a man so she could steal it back.

DIMAS. (*Aside.*) Sounds like easy money for me! (*Aloud.*) And that pretty little valet, I suppose we have to cut her in? Does *she* steal hearts too?

HARLEQUIN. I wouldn't mind stealing *hers*.

DIMAS. If you steal like you keep secrets, I don't think you could manage it.

(*LÉONIDE and CORINE appear in the distance.*)

DIMAS. But look, by God. Here they come. (*Extending his open palm to Harlequin.*) Cash down, skirts up!

(*HARLEQUIN grudgingly tosses Dimas a coin.*)

Scene 2

CORINE. (*To Léonide.*) We can't possibly talk to him when he's with that gardener.

DIMAS. (*To Harlequin.*) They seem a little shy. Tell them I already know everything there is to know about their bodies.

HARLEQUIN. (*To Léonide.*) No need for circumspection, madam. I ... am a blabbermouth.

LÉONIDE. (*Still playing Phocion.*) Who are you calling madam, Harlequin?

HARLEQUIN. *You.* I'm telling you, I let the cat out of the bag. He tricked me into it.

LÉONIDE. You *fool!* You told him who I was?

HARLEQUIN. Lock stock and bosom.

LÉONIDE. Good God!

DIMAS. I know you want to steal a heart, and I know whose heart you want to steal. And I know about Harlequin's money. The only thing I *don't* know is where is my share, because he promised me one.

LÉONIDE. Corine, that does it. My plans are completely ruined.

CORINE. Now madam, don't be discouraged. To get what *you're* after, we're going to need all the help we can get. There's nothing to do but bribe the gardener as well. Am I right, Dimas?

DIMAS. Absolutely right, mademoiselle.

CORINE. And your price?

DIMAS. I guess you'll have to pay me what I'm worth.

HARLEQUIN. He's a chiseler, and he isn't worth a sou.

LÉONIDE. That suits me fine, Dimas. Here's something in advance, and if you hold your tongue you will thank your lucky stars for having been associated with this little adventure.

DIMAS. Your servant, madam. I'm bought and sold.

HARLEQUIN. And I'm ruined! If it weren't for my damnéd tongue all that money would have made its way into *my* pockets. Do you realize that you're buying the confidence of this cutup with *my* savings?

LÉONIDE. Don't be sad, Harlequin, I'll make you *both* rich.

Now listen to me, I have a problem. A little while ago Hermocrate promised to let me stay on here a while, but I'm afraid he may have changed his mind. He is at this very moment deep in conversation about it with his sister and Agis, who want me to stay. (*Aside.*) Tell me the truth Harlequin, you didn't let anything slip to him à propos of my designs on Agis, did you?

HARLEQUIN. Certainly not, my Lady Bountiful. I told only this mercenary dog.

DIMAS. Yes you did, but you'll shut up now if you know what's good for you!

(*HARLEQUIN glares at Dimas.*)

LÉONIDE. If you haven't said anything, we have nothing to worry about. Corine, let them in on my plans for Hermocrate and the sister. You and Harlequin will handle the portraits, Dimas and I will handle the philosopher. If we don't make *very* careful arrangements ...

CORINE. Don't you worry, we'll get it right.

LÉONIDE. I see Agis. Off with you, and for God's sake don't let Hermocrate catch you together!

(*The SERVANTS hurry off together.*)

Scene 3

AGIS. *(Entering, a little out of breath.)* Ah Phocion, I've been looking for you. As you can see I'm very anxious. You see, Hermocrate seems less inclined to let you stay, but he offers no reasonable arguments, and *I* still haven't spoken even a *word* on your behalf. I just happened to be present when his sister spoke for you. She was utterly convincing, but I'm not sure what will come of it, because something urgent called Hermocrate away in the middle of their conversation. *(A beat.)* I've never been ... displeased ... with him, until today. But, my dear Phocion, don't let what I've said discourage you. You have a friend in this conspiracy. I'll speak to him, and we'll convince him yet.

LÉONIDE. Are you really my friend, Agis? Do you still find it nice to have me here?

AGIS. If you left, I expect I'd find it terribly dreary.

LÉONIDE. You're the only thing keeping me here.

AGIS. Do you really feel that way? I do, too.

LÉONIDE. A thousand times more than I can say.

AGIS. Will you give me proof? You see, this is the first time that I have tasted the excitement of ... friendship.

(LÉONIDE offers Agis her hand. HE clasps it.)

AGIS. You have initiated me. Teach me what friendship is. But please don't teach me the pain of losing a friend.

LÉONIDE. I couldn't teach you that without suffering it myself.

AGIS. That's a very good answer, I am touched by it!
Listen—remember when you said to me that only I could
decide if we would always be together?

(LÉONIDE nods yes.)

AGIS. Well here's how I see it.
LÉONIDE. Tell me.
AGIS. I won't be able to leave here in the foreseeable
future. Important matters prevent that—you'll know them
some day. But Phocion, you who are master of your fate,
I'm telling you, I shall one day be master of mine. (*A
beat.*) You simply *must* stay with us for a while. It's true
that life is lonely here, but we will be together, and what
sweeter thing can the world offer than the companionship
of two honest, loving ... hearts.
LÉONIDE. Oh Agis, I will stay, I promise. Hearing
you say this, I don't even care about the outside world. My
world will be only where you are.
AGIS. I am happy. You know, the gods cursed the hour
of my birth, and brought me into a world of ... misfortune.
But if you really do stay, they'll be kinder, I'm sure. This
is a sign of good things to come!
LÉONIDE. I am glad to see you so happy, but at the
same time I am ... apprehensive. *(A beat.)* Love can change
these tender feelings so suddenly. A friend can't compete
with a lover.
AGIS. Love? You speak to me of *love*? Phocion, may
heaven make your heart impervious to love, as it did mine!
You don't know me. My education, my sensibility, my
reason—everything closes my heart to love. It was *love*
that cursed my birth, that tainted the blood I came from. I

hate love, and I hate even the thought of the female sex, who would urge us to it.

LÉONIDE. (*With gravity.*) You mean ... you hate women?

AGIS. I will avoid women all my life.

LÉONIDE. This changes everything between us, sir. I promised you I'd stay here, but now I can't—not in good faith. It is no longer possible. I must leave. Under the circumstances you would only reproach me for staying, and as I absolutely do not wish to deceive you, I must give you back the friendship you have given me.

AGIS. What are you *saying*, Phocion? Why this sudden change? What did I say that could have offended you?

LÉONIDE. Don't worry Agis, you will not regret my leaving. You are afraid to know the pain of losing a friend? *I* will soon feel it, but you will not.

AGIS. I ... am no longer your friend?

LÉONIDE. No, you shall always be my friend; it is *I* who am no longer yours. For I am nothing more than one of those hated ... objects ... that you were speaking of a moment ago ...

AGIS. Then ... you ... are not Phocion?

LÉONIDE. No, sir. My clothes mislead you; they hide from you an unfortunate girl. My name is Aspasie, I am the last of a noble and wealthy family, and I am escaping the persecution of Princess Léonide, who wants me to give my fortune *and* my hand in marriage to a relative of hers who loves me and whom I can't abide. I was informed that on hearing of my refusal the princess decided to have me kidnapped, and the only way I could think to save myself was to take refuge in this disguise.

I had heard that Hermocrate hated the princess, and that he lived in seclusion, and I came here, without being recognized, to seek a safe haven. And then I met you. You offered me your friendship, and I could see you were completely worthy of mine. That I trust you with this secret should be proof that I have given you *my* friendship; and I will never withdraw it, even though yours will soon give way to hatred.

AGIS. I am dumbfounded, I can't unravel my thoughts.

LÉONIDE. I will unravel them for you: Hermocrate wants me gone, and now you do as well. Goodbye sir.

(SHE starts to leave.)

AGIS. No madam, wait! Your sex is not to be trusted, it is true, but ... we must be considerate of those less fortunate than ourselves.

LÉONIDE. You hate me, sir.

(SHE makes to leave again.)

AGIS. No, I'm telling you—Aspasie, stop! I feel sorry for your ... situation. I am ashamed of my insensitivity. I'll plead with Hermocrate myself, if necessary, to allow you to stay. Your predicament is ... undeniable.

LÉONIDE. So. Pity is all that's left of what you felt for me. *(Indicating her clothes.)* This ... *travesty* is so discouraging. This young prince they want me to marry is probably very nice; wouldn't it just be better to give myself up, rather than prolong this dreadful masquerade?

AGIS. I advise against it madam. It's important that when you give your hand, you also give your heart. I have always heard it said that to be married to someone one doesn't love is the saddest of all fates; that one's life becomes a web of loneliness and melancholy; that the very virtuousness that might have inspired such a decision, and in which one might seek refuge from it, in the end breaks one's spirit. (*A beat.*) But perhaps you could love this ... prince they have chosen for you ...

LÉONIDE. No sir, I couldn't. Isn't my running away proof of that?

AGIS. Then be wary of going back. Especially if you harbor any feelings of ... feelings for any other ... person. Because if you loved someone else, it would be even worse.

LÉONIDE. No, I tell you, I am like you. This is the first time that I have tasted ... how did you say it? The excitement of friendship? You have initiated *me*. And if you decide ... not to withdraw your friendship, well, that's all I could wish for.

AGIS. (*Embarrassed.*) Well if you feel that way, do not chance another encounter with Princess Léonide. Because I feel now as I did. Before.

LÉONIDE. You still love me then?

AGIS. Always madam. All the more because there's nothing to fear; there's nothing between us, except friendship, which is the only sentiment I could encourage, and undoubtedly ... also the only one you are likely to feel.

LÉONIDE and AGIS. (*Together, variously, nodding.*) Right, yes, absolutely.

LÉONIDE. Sir, no one could be worthier than you to be called Friend. Or to be called Lover, I daresay, ... though it won't be I who will call you that.

AGIS. That's something I'd never wish to be called.

LÉONIDE. Let's change the subject; it's dangerous even to speak of love.

AGIS. (*A little abashed.*) It seems the valet is looking for you. Perhaps that means Hermocrate is finished with his business. If you'll excuse me ... I think I'll go find him.

(*AGIS backs off and leaves. HARLEQUIN and CORINE enter.*)

Scene 4

HARLEQUIN. So, Mistress Phocion, your little interview was well guarded by two hungry watchdogs.

CORINE. The philosopher has not appeared, but the sister is looking for you. She looks a little sad. Apparently Hermocrate won't give in to her demands.

LÉONIDE. He will try to resist, but he will submit. Or all the art of my sex is useless.

HARLEQUIN. And does the Lord Agis show any promise? When you heat him up, does he melt?

LÉONIDE. Another little interview or two and I'll sweep him off his feet.

CORINE. Not seriously, madam?

LÉONIDE. Yes, Corine. You know the situation, and what I hope to achieve. It seems the gods approve of my love.

HARLEQUIN. And they can't help but approve of mine, because it couldn't be more innocent. (*HE throws his arms around Corine.*)

CORINE. Yes ... well ... here comes Léontine. Let's go.

LÉONIDE. Are you ready for your next scene?

CORINE. Yes, madam.

HARLEQUIN. You will be *ravished* by my performance!

(LÉONTINE appears; CORINE and HARLEQUIN bow and withdraw.)

Scene 5

LÉONIDE. I was just asking after you. They told me that Hermocrate wants to go back on the promise he made me. I am in a terrible state.

LÉONTINE. It's true, Phocion. He also refuses to keep the promise he made *me*—and with an obstinacy that seems positively irrational. I know you'll ask me to press him further, but I've come to tell you that I will do nothing more about it.

LÉONIDE. Léontine, you ...

LÉONTINE. No. His refusal has brought me to my senses again.

LÉONIDE. And you call this coming to your senses? So! My love for you blinds me, I can think only of offering myself to you, I *do* offer myself to you, I abandon myself utterly to you, I yearn to touch you yet patiently refrain from doing so—and you want me to leave you? No, Léontine, that is not possible, that is the one sacrifice I could not make for you. Where do you suggest I find the strength to *do* this? What strength have you left me?

Consider my situation! I appeal again to your virtue. Let virtue stand between us and judge our case! I am in your garden; you have suffered my presence here. You know that I love you with a passion, infinitely hot, that cuts to the core of my being, a passion awakened by you. And you want me to leave?! Ah Léontine, ask of me my life, tear out my heart—but do not expect the impossible!

LÉONTINE. Such demonstrative behavior! Such *emotion*! No Phocion, now I am *certain* that you must leave; I will not be involved in this any more. Good heavens! What would become of my heart, were it as ... *emotional* as yours? I would have always to struggle, and resist, yet never win? It is love you wish to arouse in me, isn't it? Love, and not the anguish of *feeling* love? Because that is all I *would* feel. So go! Please go away, and leave me *as I am*.

LÉONIDE. For pity's sake, be patient with me, Léontine. If I left this place I would wander blindly, lost to myself. I wouldn't know how to live without you. My grief would paralyze me. I hardly know who I *am* anymore!

LÉONTINE. And because you are devastated, I must love you? What tyranny is this?

LÉONIDE. Do you hate me?

LÉONTINE. I should!

LÉONIDE. But your heart—isn't it disposed to forgive me?

LÉONTINE. I am not listening to my heart.

LÉONIDE. Perhaps, but I am.

LÉONTINE. *(Distraught.)* Stop! Stop!

(LÉONIDE surreptitiously beckons Harlequin.)

LÉONTINE. I hear someone.

(HARLEQUIN enters.)

Scene 6

Without saying a word HARLEQUIN stands between Léonide and Léontine, and looks very closely at Léonide.

LÉONIDE. What is the valet doing here, madam?

HARLEQUIN. The master, Hermocrate, ordered me to study your behavior very closely, because he doesn't know you from Adam.

LÉONIDE. But since I am with madam, my behavior needn't be studied quite so closely. Pray tell him to go, madam.

LÉONTINE. I had better go myself.

LÉONIDE. *(Softly, to Léontine.)* If you run away without promising to intercede for me, I'm not answerable for my actions.

LÉONTINE. *(Upset.)* Run along, Harlequin, it's not necessary for you to stay.

HARLEQUIN. More necessary than you think, madam. You do not know who you're dealing with. This *gentleman* here is not so much interested in virtue as in women *of* virtue! And I'm warning you that he intends to corrupt yours ... madam!

LÉONTINE. What are you up to, Harlequin? I've had no indication that what you say is true. This must be one of your jokes.

HARLEQUIN. Ah, madam, would that it were! But listen to this: just now his valet, another rapscallion if ever I saw one, comes to me and says, "So! What say you? Let's be friends—*best* of friends! You should be glad to serve here. Honorable types, your employers. *Admirable*! Your mistress is especially obliging. A *divine* woman! Tell me, has she had many suitors?"

"As many as she's wanted," I said.

"Does she have any at the moment?"

"As many as she wants."

"Will she have more?"

"As many as she may choose to have."

"Does she desire ... marriage?"

"She doesn't tell me her desires."

(*Very pointedly.*) *"Is she a confirmed spinster?!"*

(*HE pauses for effect.*)

HARLEQUIN. "I cannot vouch for her in this matter."

"Who sees her and who doesn't? Does anyone come around? Does *no one* come around?" And on and on in this manner.

"You won't get a thing out of me," I said. "Why, is your master in love with her?"

"Out of his *mind* in love with her," came the answer. "We're only sticking around here to capture her heart, so that she'll marry us; for we have enough money, and enough lust, for *ten* marriages!"

LÉONIDE. Haven't you said enough?

HARLEQUIN. Look how I've upset him! Perhaps *he'll* tell you the rest—if you want to hear it ...

LÉONTINE. Your valet, Lord Phocion, wasn't he just amusing himself saying all that?

(SHE turns to Léonide. Total silence. Suddenly, passionately.)

LÉONTINE. *Answer* me, Phocion!

(A long beat.)

HARLEQUIN. *(To Léontine.)* Cat got your tongue, madam? You're losing your heart; it is being kidnapped even as we speak. And I am going to call Lord Hermocrate to the rescue. When love has once gangrened the soul, reason flees as though her tail were on fire! *(HE turns to go.)*

LÉONTINE. Stop Harlequin, where are you going?! He mustn't know that someone has spoken to me ... of love.

HARLEQUIN. *(A feigned revelation.)* Aha! Now that the kidnapper is a *friend* of hers, there's no need to call for help! I guess virtue is *not* its own reward after all ... Well well well. Prude goeth before a fall.

(LÉONTINE cringes.)

HARLEQUIN. So elope then! There'll always be *virtuous* women—being honest has *some* advantages!

(LÉONIDE throws Harlequin some coins, then, behind Léontine's back, motions him away.)

HARLEQUIN. (*Looking at the coins in his hand.*)
Cat's got *my* tongue now. (*To Léontine.*) I congratulate
you, madam. Goodbye. And rest assured, discretion is the
better part ... of a valet.

(*HARLEQUIN beckons Corine as HE leaves.*)

LÉONTINE. Where am I? It all seems like a dream.
Look what you've exposed me to!

(*CORINE makes noises in the background.*)

LÉONTINE. Ah, *now* who's coming?!

(*Enter CORINE.*)

Scene 7

CORINE. (*Presenting a small portrait to Léonide.*)
Here's what you asked for, sir. See if you're happy with it.
I daresay it would be even better if the subject had actually
been present while I painted.
LÉONIDE. (*Sharply.*) Why bring me this in the lady's
presence? (*Glaring at Corine.*) Well, let's have a look. Yes,
the face is just right; there's that refinement, the
selflessness—and all the fire of her eyes. And yet, I think
her actual eyes are even a little more fiery than these.
LÉONTINE. Apparently that is a portrait, sir?

LÉONIDE. (*Handing the portrait back to Corine.*) Yes, madam.

CORINE. (*Taking the portrait.*) Thank you sir, I'll work on the eyes.

(*CORINE and LÉONIDE look at Léontine's eyes.*)

LÉONTINE. Might one see it before it's whisked away?

LÉONIDE. It's not finished, madam.

LÉONTINE. Well, as you have your reasons for not wanting to show it, I won't insist.

LÉONIDE. (*Overlapping her.*) Since you insist, madam. (*Taking the portrait from Corine.*) But you must promise to give it back to me.

(*SHE gives the portrait to Léontine.*)

LÉONTINE. But ... it's of me!

LÉONIDE. I want to have you with me always. The slightest separation—even if it lasts only a moment—makes me suffer. And this portrait will alleviate my suffering. Please give it back now.

LÉONTINE. I shouldn't, but so much love makes me weak.

(*SHE gives the portrait back. LÉONIDE catches her hand.*)

LÉONIDE. Doesn't this love tempt you, even a little?

LÉONTINE. God knows I didn't want it to, but I may no longer have any choice in the matter. (*SHE weeps.*)

LÉONIDE. You don't know what joy you give me.

LÉONTINE. (*Through her tears.*) Is it decided then, that I am to love you?

LÉONIDE. Don't promise me your heart, Léontine, tell me it's mine already.

LÉONTINE. (*Very moved.*) If I did, it would be all too true. Phocion ...

LÉONIDE. I will stay then, and you will speak again to Hermocrate.

LÉONTINE. Yes. It must be so. It will give me time to reconcile myself to our ... being together.

CORINE. This meeting is now over—I see Dimas.

LÉONTINE. I don't want to be seen like this. I'm so overcome with ... feelings .... My heart .... Phocion.

(LÉONIDE and LÉONTINE look at each other.)

LÉONTINE. I will change his mind.

(LÉONTINE leaves.)

Scene 8

DIMAS. (*Entering.*) The philosopher is here, all dreamy-eyed. Leave the field to me: to plant ideas, one must have the right conditions. When I get through with him, he will be *really* cultivated.

LÉONIDE. Into the breach, Dimas!

(SHE runs off. CORINE follows her. HERMOCRATE enters.)

Scene 9

HERMOCRATE. Have you been watching Phocion?

DIMAS. Yes, and I can bring you up to date.

HERMOCRATE. Very well then, have you found anything out? Is he often with Agis? Does he seek him out?

DIMAS. Oh no, hardly. He has other things on his mind. His brain is in a stew.

HERMOCRATE. (*Aside.*) I may not want to hear the rest of this. (*Aloud.*) What things?

DIMAS. Well God in heaven, you are a wonderful man! One can only marvel at your knowledge, your morals ... your good looks.

HERMOCRATE. What has inspired this sudden enthusiasm for me?

DIMAS. Well it's just that all these goings-on make me see you in a new light. And I must tell you, astonishing things are going on—changes!—that show you to be a singular man, a very unusual man, a man so rare you're ... practically extinct! People are sighing, people are dying, people are crying out, "How I love this precious man! This *generous* man!"

(*HE throws himself on Hermocrate and hugs him fondly.*)

HERMOCRATE. Dimas! What *are* you talking about?

DIMAS. I'm talking about *you*. And of course I'm also talking about a boy who's really a girl.

HERMOCRATE. I do not know any persons of that description.

DIMAS. You know Phocion, don't you? Well, there's a woman in his pants.

HERMOCRATE. What are you saying?

DIMAS. And by God she's a charmer.

(HERMOCRATE turns sharply away.)

DIMAS. What's this face? You should be happy! Guess who she really wants to give all those charms to? I heard them talking about it. (*Proceeding slowly and carefully.*) "I'm saving myself for the most tedious of men!" No no, I've got it wrong, I made a mistake— "... saving myself for the most *fastidious*," no "*hideous* of men," yes! No!! "... for the *prettiest*," no!... "for the *wittiest* of men!" That's it! "*Hermocrate!*"

HERMOCRATE. Who, me?

DIMAS. I was following her, like you said, and she was wandering around in the bushes with her valet, Hermidas, who's about as much of a man as she is. I crept up on the other side of the bushes, and I heard them talking. "I'm done for Corine," says Phocion, "there's no curing me, my sweet. I love him too much, that man. I don't know what to do any more, or what to say."

"But madam," says the pretty little one, "he will come around. You are famous for your booty!"

"Ah, but what good is my booty if he sends me away?"

"You must be patient, madam."

"Yes but where is he? What is he doing? What is he thinking? Does he love me? What will he decide?"

HERMOCRATE. (*Moved.*) Stop, Dimas.

DIMAS. I'm almost finished. "But what does he say to you when you speak with him, madam?"

"He scolds at me, and I get upset. He speaks wisely, and I try to do the same back. 'I pity you,' he says. 'I will change,' I tell him. 'Have you no shame?' he says. 'Will shame increase my chances?' I ask him. 'But your virtue, madam.' 'Marry your virtue to mine, sir, and *cure* me!' "

HERMOCRATE. I don't need to hear any more, thank you, that's enough.

DIMAS. Well I think you should cure the child, master, by catching her illness and making *her* take care of *you.* If you never look at a woman, your ... family tree will never grow. And that would be too bad.

And along these lines, seeing as how even though I know everything I'm not going to breathe a word of it ... could you put in a good word for me with that pretty little chambermaid?

HERMOCRATE. (*Aside.*) The final indignity. (*Aloud.*) Dimas, I am ordering you to hold your tongue. It would be devastating for ... the person in question, if this story got around. I am going to send these women away. Order must be restored!

(*Exit HERMOCRATE, sighing audibly. LÉONIDE returns quietly.*)

Scene 10

LÉONIDE. So, Dimas, what is he thinking?

DIMAS. He says your wardrobe must be restored. So he's sending you away.

LÉONIDE. I thought as much.

DIMAS. But then, I think he wants to keep you.

LÉONIDE. You've lost me.

DIMAS. What's worse, he seems to have lost himself. He can't make out what he wants at all. "Ah ...." That was the last thing he said. All his philosophy has dried up, there's hardly any left.

LÉONIDE. Well what *is* left he'll surrender to me. He may be wise, but he'll fall into the same trap that caught his sister.

Meanwhile I'm worried that Agis is avoiding me. I haven't seen him at all since he found out that I'm a woman. But look. I see him speaking to Corine. Maybe he's trying to find me.

DIMAS. You know him through and through—here he comes.

(HE turns to go but hesitates and turns back.)

DIMAS. Madam, all this double-dealing—it won't leopardize my fortune, will it?

LÉONIDE. *(Smiling.)* No. Your fortune is safe.

DIMAS. *(From his heart.)* Thank you so much.

(DIMAS leaves. AGIS enters. LÉONIDE turns to go.)

Scene 11

AGIS. Aspasie! You run away from me every time I come near.

LÉONIDE. The fact is you ran away from me when last we spoke.

AGIS. I admit it. But I was troubled by something, something ... disquieting. And it won't leave me alone.

LÉONIDE. Will you tell me about it?

(A long beat.)

AGIS. *(Haltingly.)* There is a person ... I am very drawn to, but I cannot ascertain if what I feel is friendship or love. All this is so new to me—I must ask you again to advise me, to give me some ... instruction.

LÉONIDE. I think I can guess who this person is.

AGIS. That couldn't be hard. You know that when you came here I had never loved at all. And since you've been here, I've hardly looked at anyone but you. So it follows, logically, that ...

LÉONIDE. The person is ... I.

(A beat.)

AGIS . Yes, it's you Aspasie. Can you tell me what I should make of it?

LÉONIDE. I can't help you at all. Maybe you can tell me what *I* should make of it. Because I am in the same ... predicament. When I came here *I* had never loved at all. And since coming here I've hardly looked at anyone but you. And I have changed, too.

(A beat.)

AGIS. You love me, Aspasie.

LÉONIDE. Yes, but what have we really learned from this? We loved each other first as friends, *then* we started feeling confused. Do we love each other now as we did first? Or in a different way? That's what we need to know.

AGIS. Perhaps we could figure it out if we told each other what we are feeling.

LÉONIDE. All right, let's see.

(*After some thought.*) Did you have difficulty avoiding me just now?

AGIS. Immense difficulty.

LÉONIDE. This does not bode well. Did you avoid me because your heart was troubled by feelings you didn't dare tell me about?

AGIS. (*Delighted.*) That's it exactly! You understand me so well.

LÉONIDE. Well there you are. But I'm warning you, you're not necessarily going to feel *better* because of all this. In fact, from what I see in your eyes, the prognosis is less than promising.

AGIS. My eyes look at you with the greatest of pleasure—with a pleasure bordering on ... excitement.

LÉONIDE. Well. That could only be real love. It isn't necessary to ask *you* any more questions.

AGIS. I would give my life for you. I'd give a thousand if I had them.

LÉONIDE. The case is closed. Love in your words, love in your eyes, love in your heart. This is real love if ever there was love, love as it ought to be ... as it has always been.

AGIS. Or perhaps ... as it has never been. (*A beat.*) So you can see, Aspasie, I love you not as I first did, but in a very different way. Now that you know what is happening in my heart, oughtn't I to know what is happening in yours?

LÉONIDE. Be careful Agis. A person of my sex may talk as much as she likes about her friendships, but must never speak of her love. Besides, you are already too full of tenderness, too ... naked with tenderness; if you were to expose *my* heart's desire, things could get even worse than they already are.

AGIS. You were talking about my eyes, let's talk about yours. They seem to be telling me something new about your love for me.

LÉONIDE. I can't answer for my eyes. They may well tell you that my love for you has deepened. But I suppose I don't mind telling you that myself.

AGIS. (*Overwhelmed.*) Oh God—your words throw me into an abyss ... of *passion*! Unfathomable! Incredible! You feel as I do!

LÉONIDE. Yes, it's true. I can't help myself. But to love as we love—it isn't enough. One must have the freedom to *live* one's love, and to be able to go on living it, and speaking it, forever. And Lord Hermocrate, who makes the rules ...

AGIS. (*Interrupting her.*) I respect Hermocrate, and I love him, Aspasie, but I am beginning to learn that the heart cannot live by rules. I must see him immediately, before he finds you; he may already have decided to send you away, and we will need a little time to figure out ... what we are going to do.

DIMAS. (*Appears upstage and hovers there, singing a warning.*) Tra la la la la.

LÉONIDE. You're right, Agis. You should go, quickly—but let's find each other again soon. I have so much to say to you.

AGIS. (*Exuberant.*) And I to you!

LÉONIDE. Go! Leave! When people see us together I'm afraid they'll be able to read my thoughts, and see exactly who I am.

AGIS. A bientôt, my beautiful Aspasie. This time I am going to find Hermocrate, and convince him!

(HE races away.)

Scene 12

DIMAS. (*Speaking hurriedly.*) By God, he's lucky he got away. The jealous one is here!

(HE moves off quickly as HERMOCRATE enters.)

LÉONIDE. Hermocrate! Out of hiding at last. Couldn't you think of any other way to dampen my ardor than by *avoiding* me? And leaving me anxious and melancholy? Well your strategy hasn't worked; it makes me sadder, but no less loving.

HERMOCRATE. No, in fact something else kept me away, Aspasie. But I'm afraid your feelings are no longer at issue. Your presence here, from this moment on, is really ... unmanageable. And it can only hurt you. Dimas knows who you are. Need I say more? He knows your ... heart's desire. He overheard you talking, and neither you nor I can afford to count on the discretion of someone like that. So you must leave for your own good, to protect your honor.

LÉONIDE. Leave, sir? Would you send me away in this state—a thousand times more confused than when I came here? What have you done to cure me? Is this the lesson in self-denial for which I sought out the wise Hermocrate?

HERMOCRATE. I hope what I have to say will end your confusion. You thought me wise. You loved me for that reason. But I am not at all wise. A truly wise and virtuous person would not be threatened by your presence. Do you know why I am sending you away? Because I am afraid that your secret will expose me, and make people think less of me. Because I am proud, and I fear that I won't *seem* virtuous—without troubling myself meanwhile to *be* virtuous. Because I am nothing but a vain and arrogant man, to whom wisdom is less important than the contemptible, deceitful mockery he has made of it. This, then, is the object of your love.

LÉONIDE. I have never admired it so much.

HERMOCRATE. You *can't* be serious.

LÉONIDE. Oh but I am, my lord. That you can confess these things makes you even stronger—and me even weaker. You say you are not at all wise, and then you provide splendid proof that the opposite is true. This strategy isn't going to work either.

HERMOCRATE. Wait, madam. You believed me capable of feeling all that love lets loose in the hearts of other men. Do you remember when you said that? Well, the least civilized soul, the most common lover, the most impulsive youth could not experience more upsetting emotions than those I have been feeling—nervousness, dread, rapture, jealousy. Is this a proper portrait of

Hermocrate? The world is full of men who *want* to feel these things; any man picked at random is more suitable for this love of yours than I, madam. *You must not feel it for me!*

LÉONIDE. But I do. You tell me to protect my honor: could there be a greater honor than inspiring in you the feelings of which you speak? Or than that which you do me when you speak of them? *You* are protecting my honor! I no longer need ask you to help me find peace of mind; your confession has given it to me. I am at peace, I am happy. You have pledged yourself to me. We belong to each other.

HERMOCRATE. Then there's only one thing left to say—and I will end with that. If you stay, I will reveal your secret; the man you so admire will be disgraced; and his disgrace will reflect very poorly on you, and forever haunt your conscience.

LÉONIDE. And if I leave, my revenge will be certain— the love you feel for me will take care of that. I leave, and you run away from a love that could have been the sweet salvation of your life, and which will be the ruination of mine. I leave, and you delight in your sacred Reason, your relentless wisdom—fed by my unhappiness they will surely thrive. I leave, and you destroy my heart.

I came to ask you for help in conquering my love for you, but you have given me no help at all, aside from admitting that you love me—an admission that redoubles *my* love. And after this, you send me away. Your so-called wisdom shores itself up at the expense of a young heart whose trust you have betrayed, whose virtuous intentions you have not respected at all, and which has served only as fodder to your rigidly held opinions and heartless theories.

Surely my shame will reflect poorly on *you* and haunt *your* conscience!

HERMOCRATE. Lower your voice, madam. Someone is coming.

LÉONIDE. (*Louder.*) You torment me, and expect me to keep my voice down?!

HERMOCRATE. (*Turning sharply to her, shouting her down.*) You move me more than you think! (*A beat. In a passionate whisper.*) But kindly *do not speak in a loud voice*!

(*HARLEQUIN enters, followed by CORINE.*)

Scene 13

CORINE. (*Running after Harlequin.*) Give that back to me! What right do you have to steal it? What are you *doing*?!

HARLEQUIN. What the devil do you *think* I'm doing? Would you make a mockery of my loyalty?! I am going to inform the master!

HERMOCRATE. (*To Harlequin.*) What is all this noise? What's the matter here?

HARLEQUIN. The matter here is one of some consequence to you, and only these devils know the details. However, since I have unmanned them, we'll soon know everything.

HERMOCRATE. Unmanned them?

HARLEQUIN. I just found this little fellow striking the pose of a thinker. He mused dreamily, he shook his head feverishly, he examined his manuscript intently. And I noticed he had at his side this shell, covered with green, yellow, gray and white, where he dipped his pen. I sneaked up on him to see what document he was forging, but what a rogue! He wasn't forging words or letters, he was forging a *face*! And that face, sir, was yours.

HERMOCRATE. Mine!

HARLEQUIN. Your very face, except for the fact that it was a lot less, well ... *large* than the one you are wearing at the moment. Why just the *nose* that you normally have on is bigger than your entire face in this pretty little portrait! Is that legal? To belittle someone so? To cut him down to size? Look what this headshrinker has *done* to you—look at your *expression*!

(HE thrusts the portrait at Hermocrate.)

HERMOCRATE. (*Taking the portrait.*) Bravo, Harlequin. I don't blame you at all for being suspicious. Run along. I will look into this.

HARLEQUIN. Make them give you back the rest of yourself. You can't save face if you're missing most of it.

(HE stalks off.)

Scene 14

HERMOCRATE. (*To Corine.*) Why did you paint me? What were you after?

CORINE. I was glad to make a portrait of an illustrious man, and I would be proud to show it to people. It seemed a natural thing, sir.

HERMOCRATE. You flatter me.

CORINE. And besides, I knew that this portrait would give pleasure to someone in particular, who would never have ventured to commission it.

HERMOCRATE. And who is that someone?

CORINE. Sir, I ...

LÉONIDE. Hold your tongue, Corine.

HERMOCRATE. What's going on here? Aspasie?

LÉONIDE. Don't press her any further. Let's just pretend this never happened.

HERMOCRATE. (*Looking at the portrait.*) Yes but it *has* happened, how can I ignore it?

LÉONIDE. (*Sounding distraught.*) Let's not *talk* about it any more. You are embarrassing me. (*SHE covers her face with her hands.*)

HERMOCRATE. (*Clutching the portrait.*) I can't believe what I am seeing. Or what is happening to me. (*Struggling to contain himself.*) *I don't know any more what is happening to me.*

LÉONIDE. (*With passion.*) I don't know if I can endure any more of this!

HERMOCRATE. (*Overlapping her, confounded.*) This is .... I am under a spell. I am being swept away.

LÉONIDE. Ah Corine, why have you *done* this?!

HERMOCRATE. Have you triumphed, Aspasie? Have you won the day?

(*A beat. The WOMEN are beside themselves with expectation.*)

HERMOCRATE. I *surrender*!

LÉONIDE. You are embarrassing me again, but I cannot hold it against you.

HERMOCRATE. Take the portrait back. It belongs to you, madam.

LÉONIDE. I will not take it back unless your heart comes with it.

(THEY stand very close together.)

HERMOCRATE. It does. Nothing must keep you from having it. (*A beat.*) Take it from me.

(LÉONIDE takes the portrait and hands it behind her back to CORINE, who hands her a portrait of LÉONIDE in its stead.)

LÉONIDE. (*Offering Hermocrate the portrait of herself.*) Then nothing must keep *you* from having *this*. (*A beat.*) Take it from me.

(HERMOCRATE takes it.)

HERMOCRATE. It is of you.

LÉONIDE. Show me that you cherish it.

(HERMOCRATE presses it slowly to his lips.)

HERMOCRATE. Have I humbled myself enough? I will not argue with you any more.

CORINE. (*Studying Hermocrate's portrait.*) There's still something not quite right about it .... But if the master will stand very still for a moment, I can fix it straightaway.

LÉONIDE. Since we are alone and it will take only a moment, please don't refuse, my lord.

HERMOCRATE. (*Standing very still.*) Aspasie, we are running a risk; someone could catch us together.

LÉONIDE. If as you say this is my moment of triumph, let's not throw it away—it's too precious. (*Backing slowly away.*) Your eyes look at me with a tenderness I would like to keep with me forever—so I can savor the memory. (*Moving out of Hermocrate's sight.*) You cannot see your eyes, sir. They are enchanted.

Quickly, Corine! Finish!

CORINE. Could you move your head a little to the side, sir?

(*HERMOCRATE turns his head, looking for Léonide.*)

CORINE. No, towards *me,* sir.

HERMOCRATE. Dear God, what are you reducing me to?

LÉONIDE. (*Close behind Hermocrate.*) Does your heart blush at what you would do for me?

HERMOCRATE. Do you wish it, Aspasie?

CORINE. Turn a touch to the right.

HERMOCRATE. (*In a hushed voice.*) Stop, here comes Agis! Go, Hermidas!

(*Alarmed, THEY leap into action. CORINE gathers her things and escapes. AGIS enters.*)

Scene 15

AGIS. I was coming to ask you, sir, to allow Phocion to stay with us for a while, but it seems that you may already have given your consent, and that my intervention is no longer necessary.

HERMOCRATE. (*In an anxious tone.*) You want him to stay then, Agis?

AGIS. I confess that I would have been annoyed to see him go, and that nothing could give me as much pleasure as having him stay on. To know him is to admire him, and friendship follows admiration naturally enough.

HERMOCRATE. I had no idea you were already so taken with each other.

(A beat.)

LÉONIDE. Actually, we hardly know each other.

AGIS. Apparently I am interrupting a private conversation. I beg your pardon.

(AGIS withdraws.)

Scene 16

HERMOCRATE. Agis seems quite keen on your company. I'm not sure what to think. Since he has been with me, I've never seen anything interest him as much as you seem to. Have you told him who you are? Perhaps you're leading me on.

LÉONIDE. My lord, you don't know what joy you give me! You said you'd been jealous, but I'd never *seen* you jealous—until now. I am so *glad* that you wrong me in this way. Hermocrate is jealous! He cherishes me! He *loves* me! He loves me at a price, but what does that matter?

But still I must prove my innocence. Agis has not gone far, I can still see him. Let's call him back, my lord. I'm going to speak to him *in front of you,* and you will see if I deserve your suspicions.

HERMOCRATE. No don't call him back. Aspasie, I see that I'm wrong. I give up. Your candor reassures me. And in any case, no one must know that I love you—yet. Give me time to arrange everything.

LÉONIDE. Take whatever time you need. Here is your sister. I will leave you together.

(SHE moves away.)

LÉONIDE. *(Aside.)* He is weak now. And I pity him.

(A beat.)

LÉONIDE. Heaven forgive my deception.

(SHE leaves.)

Scene 17

LÉONTINE. (*Entering.*) Ah, here you are, dear brother. I've been looking for you everywhere.

HERMOCRATE. What can I do for you, Léontine?

LÉONTINE. Where do you stand with Phocion? Do you still intend to send him away? He does go on about you so, saying *such* nice things, that I promised him he could stay and that you would consent to it. Now I gave him my word—he won't stay long, so it simply isn't worth the trouble of going back on my promise.

HERMOCRATE. No Léontine, you know my esteem for you, and I will not go against your wish. Since you promised him, I have nothing more to say about it. He can stay as long as he wants, my dear.

LÉONTINE. Thank you for being so good-natured, brother. In fact, you know, Phocion truly deserves our ... indulgence.

HERMOCRATE. I know. He does.

LÉONTINE. And moreover, I think he serves as a suitable distraction for Agis, who is at an age when he might easily rebel against his ... solitary life.

HERMOCRATE. That could happen at any age.

LÉONTINE. You're right. We all have these feelings of ... well, melancholy. (*A beat.*) I often feel quite ... bored. I hope it's not wrong to say this to you.

HERMOCRATE. Wrong? Who wouldn't get a bit bored sometimes? Are we not made for society and mutual fellowship?

LÉONTINE. You know ... it's a big step, to close oneself off from the world, in a retreat. We were perhaps quick to choose such a hard life.

(A beat.)

HERMOCRATE. Go on. I couldn't put all this into words as easily as you do.

LÉONTINE. But remember—what's done *can* be undone. One's ... circumstances can always change.

HERMOCRATE. Indeed they can!

LÉONTINE. A man of your standing would be welcome anywhere, should he wish to change his circumstances.

HERMOCRATE. And *you,* who are lovely and younger than I—I wouldn't be concerned about you, either.

LÉONTINE. Indeed brother, few *young* men can hold a candle to you, and the gift of your heart would not be taken lightly.

HERMOCRATE. And I assure you that you could receive many such gifts without making the least effort.

LÉONTINE. Then, you wouldn't be surprised if I had ... certain prospects?

HERMOCRATE. I've always been surprised that you had none.

LÉONTINE. Listen to you! And why couldn't *you* also have some?

HERMOCRATE. Well, one never knows. Perhaps I already do.

LÉONTINE. I would be *so* delighted if you did. After all, and I've thought about this carefully, is our beloved reason greater than that of the gods, who thought up marriage in the first place? I mean, a married man is just as good as an unmarried one. *(A beat.)* Well, it's good to think about these things. We'll talk about it more another time. Adieu.

HERMOCRATE. I have some things to see to; I'll be along shortly.

(LÉONTINE departs. HERMOCRATE reflects.)

HERMOCRATE. We both seem to be doing quite well for ourselves. (*HE thinks.*) On whom could she possibly have set her sights? (*HE thinks.*) I wonder if it's someone as young for her as Aspasie is for me. (*HE thinks.*) Well, we must fulfill our destinies. (*A long beat.*) How weak we are. We are so weak.

(A beat.)

BLACKOUT

ACT III

Scene 1

LÉONIDE and CORINE are discovered thinking.

LÉONIDE. Come talk to me Corine! Would you ever have believed that you and I could have done this? Hermocrate and his sister have become obsessed with me, first one, then the other, and they are both actually planning to *marry* me. In *secret*! God knows what arrangements have already been made for all these imaginary nuptials! Everything seems to point to success.

Well *I* never would have believed it—that love could reduce a famous rationalist to a passionate, jealous lover. That love could completely confound the minds of these oh-so-controlled paragons of reason and virtue. And I had to listen to every single word out of them, because I caught them as they fell ... as I must continue to do until everything is settled, finally, with Agis.

(Sighing.) Agis. I have to tell him who I am. And I dread it, but at least I know he wants to see me as much as I want to see him. He truly loves me as Aspasie, could he really hate me as Léonide?

CORINE. Take heart, madam! After all that she's done for him, Léonide would have to seem even more loveable than Aspasie.

LÉONIDE. I'm inclined to think so, but his family— his parents—were destroyed by mine.

CORINE. Your father *inherited* his throne, he did not usurp it.

LÉONIDE. What's the difference to Agis? Oh Corine, I'm so in love ... and I'm so afraid. Yet I must proceed as if I'm totally confident. (*A beat.*) Anyway, have you sent my letters home?

CORINE. Yes madam, Dimas found me a messenger. You should have an answer soon. What is the plan?

LÉONIDE. I wrote Ariston to follow the messenger back here, and to bring my guardsmen and my ceremonial carriage with him. Agis must leave this place as a proper prince. I will wait here; come and tell me the instant they arrive. That will be the crowning moment, Corine.

Thank you for all you've done for me.

CORINE. I'm off, but you're not through. (*Pointing offstage.*) She's back.

(*Enter LÉONTINE. CORINE leaves.*)

Scene 2

LÉONTINE. A word with you, my Phocion. (*Confidentially.*) The die is cast. Our troubles will soon be over.

LÉONIDE. Thank heavens.

LÉONTINE. I have taken my life into my own hands. We will be wed, we will be together forever. I still think it's wrong to have the ceremony here, yet the other arrangements you've made don't seem ... well, quite appropriate. You sent for a carriage to meet us, isn't that so? Close to the house?

(LÉONIDE nods yes.)

LÉONTINE. But wouldn't it be better if, instead of leaving together, I left alone, went ahead to the city, and awaited you there?

LÉONIDE. Yes, yes, you're right. You should go on ahead, good thinking.

LÉONTINE. I'll go immediately and get ready to leave.

(SHE starts off but suddenly stops and looks around the garden.)

LÉONTINE. Two hours from now I will no longer be here. Phocion, you will follow me soon?

LÉONIDE. *(Impatient.)* I can't follow until you've gone somewhere.

LÉONTINE. You should be grateful for my love.

LÉONIDE. Your love is ... priceless. You shouldn't make light of mine.

LÉONTINE. You are the only person in the world for whom I would take this step.

LÉONIDE. It's not so big a step as you think. You run no risk. Now go get ready.

LÉONTINE. I love your eagerness. May it last forever!

LÉONIDE. If only you were as eager. This delaying makes me impatient.

(A beat.)

LÉONTINE. I'm sorry. Sometimes a sort of fear and melancholy come over me.

LÉONIDE. Isn't it a little late for that? I feel joy, only joy.

LÉONTINE. Oh don't be impatient, I'll go now.

(SHE turns to go, sees HERMOCRATE coming, and veers off in a new direction.)

LÉONTINE. It's Hermocrate! I just *can't* see him now!

(SHE escapes, as HERMOCRATE appears.)

Scene 3

LÉONIDE. So ... Hermocrate. I thought you were busy arranging for our departure.

HERMOCRATE. Ah, my beautiful Aspasie, if only you knew how I ... must battle my demons.

LÉONIDE. Ah, and if only you knew how tired I am of battling them with you! What does it all mean? I can never be sure of anything with you.

HERMOCRATE. Forgive this uncertainty in a man whose heart should be more resolute.

LÉONIDE. (*Pointedly.*) And more ardent. Well, you can be as uncertain as you like, but you really must get ready to leave. Unless you want to stay here and have Harlequin marry us.

HERMOCRATE. No no.

(A beat. HE exhales his frustration.)

LÉONIDE. Sighing won't hasten our departure.

HERMOCRATE. I have one thing yet to say to you—it's troubling me terribly.

LÉONIDE. You never stop, there's always one thing more to say.

HERMOCRATE. Aspasie. I have surrendered everything to you—my heart, my way of life, my volition. May I keep nothing of my own?

LÉONIDE. What would you keep?

HERMOCRATE. I have raised Agis since he was eight years old. *(Struggling with his feelings.)* I cannot give him up yet. Let him come with us, let him live with us for a while.

LÉONIDE. I see ... and who *is* he? Why is he so important to you?

HERMOCRATE. *(Hesitating.)* What concerns me must now concern you. So I will tell you his secret. You have heard of King Cleomenes?

(LÉONIDE nods yes. A beat.)

HERMOCRATE. Agis is his son. He was born in a dungeon. He was smuggled out of prison shortly thereafter. I am his guardian.

LÉONIDE. His secret is in good hands.

HERMOCRATE. Imagine the care with which I have hidden him, the love I have given him ... and what would become of him if he fell into the hands of Princess Léonide. She is trying to find him, you know. Apparently she will not breathe freely until he is dead.

LÉONIDE. Yet she is widely considered to be generous, and fair.

HERMOCRATE. I put no faith in hearsay. She was born to blood that is neither generous nor fair.

LÉONIDE. They also say that she would marry the lost prince if only she knew where to find him. I mean, they are the same age ...

HERMOCRATE. Even if she chose to pursue that course, the justifiable hatred Agis feels for her would certainly prevent it from happening.

LÉONIDE. I would have thought that forgiving an enemy was worth as much as hating her—or him. Especially if that enemy has done one no harm.

HERMOCRATE. If the price of such forgiveness were not a throne, you would be right. But forgiveness at that price ...

(HE pauses, and continues icily.)

HERMOCRATE. ... is not affordable. At any rate, it's not even a consideration.

LÉONIDE. I will welcome Agis and offer him my tenderest love.

HERMOCRATE. Thank you so much. He won't be with us for long. Our allies at court are rallying secretly against the princess, and he will soon join them. Things are moving forward; we may soon see a complete turnaround at court.

LÉONIDE. Do they plan to kill the princess?

HERMOCRATE. Avenge one crime with another? She is only the heir of the wrongdoers. No, Agis would not be capable of that. It will be enough to subdue her.

LÉONIDE. Well I think you have said what you had to say to me. Go get ready to leave.

HERMOCRATE. Adieu, beloved Aspasie. (*Looking around wistfully.*) These are my last hours in this place.

(*After a moment HE leaves.*)

Scene 4

LÉONIDE. (*Peering about.*) Agis. Will he come to me now? I know he is waiting to find the right moment to speak to me. (*A beat.*) That he could hate me frightens me.

(*HARLEQUIN and DIMAS arrive in high spirits.*)

HARLEQUIN. Your servant, madam.

DIMAS. Your obedient servant, madam.

LÉONIDE. A little quieter, please.

DIMAS. Don't be suspenseful. We are alone.

LÉONIDE. What do you want?

HARLEQUIN. A bagatelle, madam.

DIMAS. We're just here to strike a balance.

HARLEQUIN. To see what we amount to.

LÉONIDE. I'm feeling a bit anxious. I haven't time for idle chat.

DIMAS. So then, have we done a good job?

LÉONIDE. Yes, you've both served me well.

DIMAS. And the seeds we planted—they are sprouting?

LÉONIDE. (*Impatient, pointing offstage.*) I am waiting to speak with Agis, who is waiting patiently for me.

HARLEQUIN. Well if he's waiting patiently for you, you needn't feel anxious.

DIMAS. And we can talk business. Well, we've sold them short. We've taken them all in.

HARLEQUIN. We were rapscallions beyond compare!

DIMAS. We were deaf to the voice of conscience. It was hard. We were brave.

HARLEQUIN. Sometimes you were a boy, and it wasn't even true! Sometimes you were a girl, and I didn't even know it!

DIMAS. There were rendezvous—sometimes with *him,* sometimes with *her.* I had to give your heart to everyone, and yet give it to no one.

HARLEQUIN. There were portraits—to trap loving faces you couldn't have cared less about, faces that thought their likenesses had real value.

LÉONIDE. *(Unamused.)* You may now get to the point.

DIMAS. Your passion play is almost over. How much is the climax worth to you?

HARLEQUIN. Would you like to buy the dénouement? We are selling it for a reasonable price.

DIMAS. Bargain with us, or we'll ruin the ending.

LÉONIDE. But didn't I promise to make your fortunes?

DIMAS. We want ready money!

HARLEQUIN. Yes, because when one no longer has use for servants, one pays them badly.

LÉONIDE. Children. How insolent we are.

DIMAS. We have a right to be!

HARLEQUIN. Insolence agrees with us!

LÉONIDE. If you stand in my way, if you are indiscreet, I will see to it that you pay for your

indiscretions in a dungeon. And I promise you, I have the
power to make that happen. If on the other hand you keep
your mouths shut, I will make good on all previous
promises. What will it be? Prison? Or money? Now I *order*
you to make yourselves scarce. You *might* redeem
yourselves with prompt obedience.

(SHE glares at them. DIMAS shrinks a little.)

DIMAS. *(To Harlequin.)* What do we do? More
insolence?
HARLEQUIN. No, dungeons are cold. Let's go.

(THEY go. AGIS enters.)

Scene 5

AGIS. I've found you, Aspasie, and we can talk. This
whole situation has caused me such *distress*! I found myself
almost hating Hermocrate and Léontine for all the affection
they seem to feel for you. I was jealous! But who wouldn't
love you? God, you are so beautiful Aspasie. And how
exquisitely sweet it is to love you.
LÉONIDE. And how it pleases me to hear you say that,
Agis. You will soon know the *real* price of that love. Tell
me ... your love is so pure, so unquestioning—is there
nothing that could take it away from me?
AGIS. Nothing. You will lose me only when I stop
breathing.

LÉONIDE. I haven't told you everything, Agis. You don't know who I am yet.

AGIS. I know your beauty. I know your heart. I will adore you until my dying moment; nothing could break your spell.

LÉONIDE. Oh Gods, such love! But the dearer it is to me, the more I am afraid to lose it.

I have kept it from you, Agis—who I really am. My name .... (*A beat.*) It may shock you.

AGIS. But Aspasie you don't know who *I* am either! Or how daunted I am by the thought of burdening your destiny with mine. (*Crying out in pain.*) Oh cruel princess, I have so many reasons to hate you!

LÉONIDE. Who are you talking about?

AGIS. Princess Léonide, Aspasie. My enemy and yours.

(*AGIS sees someone coming and spins. LÉONIDE looks to see who it is.*)

AGIS. But someone's coming! I can't continue now.

LÉONIDE. Hermocrate! I *hate* him for interrupting us. (*Turning to Agis with great focus.*) Our future depends yet on a single word. You do not realize it, but you hate me.

AGIS. Hate you?!

LÉONIDE. (*A frantic whisper.*) There's no time now. See what he wants.

(*LÉONIDE exits quickly.*)

Scene 6

AGIS. I can't imagine what she means.

(A long beat. AGIS considers the state of his affairs.)

AGIS. I don't know if I could forgive myself if I didn't tell Hermocrate what is happening to me.

(HE paces back and forth animatedly.)

Scene 7

HERMOCRATE. *(Entering.)* Wait Prince, I need to talk to you. *(A beat.)* I don't know where to begin.

AGIS. What is troubling you, sir?

HERMOCRATE. Something you probably never would have imagined, something I am ashamed to admit to you. But something I've decided, after much reflection, I must tell you.

AGIS. What is wrong?

HERMOCRATE. I am weak—as weak as any other man.

AGIS. What weakness do you refer to, sir?

HERMOCRATE. The one we forgive in every man, the most ordinary failing, the weakness one would least expect to find in me. You know my views on that emotion called love.

AGIS. It seems to me they've always been a bit extreme.

HERMOCRATE. Yes, that could well be. But can I be blamed? A solitary man given to contemplation and study, a man who communes only with his mind and never with his heart, a man imprisoned by his own opinions is hardly in a position to pass judgment on certain ... freedoms. He will always protest too much.

AGIS. There's no doubting it, you always were prone to excess.

HERMOCRATE. You are right, I agree with you! I said all kinds of things. That such intense emotion was ridiculous, extravagant, unworthy of a man of reason. I called it a delusion, and I did not know what I was saying. My words owed nothing to reason, or to nature, or to whichever God may have given us life.

AGIS. Because, deep down, we are made for loving.

HERMOCRATE. Indeed we are. Everything turns on this ... love.

AGIS. One day it may turn on *you* for having held it in such contempt.

HERMOCRATE. It has already done so.

AGIS. Really?

HERMOCRATE. Ah, I suppose I must tell you the whole of it. (*A beat.*) I am about to change my ... circumstances, and I hope you will follow me ... if you love me. I leave today. I'm going to be married.

AGIS. And that is what was troubling you?

HERMOCRATE. It's not easy to go back on a lifetime of vows; it is a big change.

AGIS. Well I congratulate you. Perhaps you needed to learn the wisdom of the heart.

HERMOCRATE. I am certainly learning a lesson. And I will not delude myself any more. If you knew what an abundance of love, what dedicated, even insistent passion this person has surprised me with, you would think poorly of me if I didn't accept them. Reason does not mean that we should be ungrateful, yet that's what I would have been.

This person sees me a few times in the forest, takes a fancy to me, tries to forget this fancy but cannot, decides to talk to me, but is intimidated by my reputation for severity. So to avoid an unpleasant reception she takes on a disguise and changes her *sex*, becoming the most beautiful young man imaginable. She arrives here, and I recognize her from my walk in the woods yesterday. I ask her to leave. I even suspect that it is *you* she wants, but she swears that isn't so, and to convince me she whispers, "I love you." (*A beat.*) "You don't believe me? I give you my hand, I give you my fortune, I give you my heart. Give me yours in return, or else cure mine of this affliction. Submit to these emotions I feel for you, or else teach me to master them. Share my love, or else give me back my freedom!" And she says all this so beguilingly, and with eyes so ... searching, and a voice so soft with love—she could subdue a savage!

AGIS. (*Disquieted.*) But sir, this tender lover in disguise—have I seen her here? Did she come *here*?

HERMOCRATE. Yes, and she's *still* here.

AGIS. But only Phocion has come here.

HERMOCRATE. (*Delighted.*) She *is* Phocion!

(*HE sees LÉONTINE coming.*)

HERMOCRATE. (*A sudden whisper.*) But don't say a word. It's Léontine.

(*LÉONTINE approaches. AGIS hides his distress.*)

Scene 8

LÉONTINE. *(To Hermocrate.)* Dear brother, I am going to make a short trip to the city.

HERMOCRATE. Indeed? And where will you be staying?

LÉONTINE. At Phrosine's. I've had news from her; she's asked me to come at once.

HERMOCRATE. Then we shall both be *in absentia.* I'm also leaving—in about an hour. I was just telling Agis.

LÉONTINE. You, too, dear brother? And where will *you* be going?

HERMOCRATE. I'm going to see Criton.

LÉONTINE. Heavens! To the city. Like me. It's ... curious that we both have business in the city. Do you remember the subject of our conversation a while ago? Your trip doesn't by any chance have some secret purpose?

HERMOCRATE. Now the way you say that makes me wonder about *your* trip. You remember what you were hinting at when we spoke.

LÉONTINE. Hermocrate, let's speak openly. We see through each other. I'm not going to see Phrosine at all.

HERMOCRATE. *(With a smile.)* Well since we are speaking frankly, I will be no less candid with you. I'm not going to see Criton.

LÉONTINE. It's my heart that leads me where I'm going.

HERMOCRATE. And mine leads me.

LÉONTINE. And what is more ... I am getting married.

(A beat.)

HERMOCRATE. Well ... so am I.

LÉONTINE. Well that's wonderful, Hermocrate! Now that we have told our secrets, perhaps my ... intended, and I, can avoid the expense of traveling elsewhere for the ceremony. He is here, and since you know everything, it's hardly necessary to sneak off.

HERMOCRATE. You're right. And I won't leave either. We will all four be married at the same time! Because she ... the one to whom I have given myself ... is also here.

LÉONTINE. (*A little perplexed.*) I haven't seen a woman here. (*A beat. Shaking off her hesitation and forging ahead cheerfully.*) *I* am marrying Phocion.

HERMOCRATE. Phocion!

LÉONTINE. Yes. Phocion.

HERMOCRATE. Well ... now ... you don't mean ... the boy who came here to study? The one who wants to stay on with us?

LÉONTINE. I don't know any other Phocion.

HERMOCRATE. No wait a minute, wait. I'm also marrying him. We can't *both* marry him.

LÉONTINE. You're marrying *him*?! That's absolutely mad!

HERMOCRATE. It's absolutely *true*.

LÉONTINE. What can this mean? *My* Phocion, the Phocion who loves me with an infinite tenderness, the one who had my portrait made without my even knowing it?

HERMOCRATE. Your portrait? That's not *your* portrait, it's *mine*! And it was without *my* even knowing it that he had it made! *She*. Did.

LÉONTINE. Are you sure you're not mistaken? (*Producing the portrait Léonide gave her.*) Look, here is *his* portrait. Do you recognize him?

HERMOCRATE. Oh my sister, I have one too.

(*HE produces his, looks at hers.*)

HERMOCRATE. Yours is of a man, mine is of a woman....

(*THEY study the little pictures intently together for a moment.*)

HERMOCRATE. But that seems to be the only difference.

LÉONTINE. (*Sadly.*) Oh heavens .... Has this happened?

AGIS. Oh, it has happened. And now I must speak. She didn't give me a portrait, but I am *also* supposed to marry her.

HERMOCRATE. What? You too, Agis? (*Grimly.*) What a very peculiar coincidence.

LÉONTINE. I am *outraged*!

HERMOCRATE. (*To Léontine.*) There's no point in grumbling. Our servants have obviously been bought, and I fear there may be more surprises in store. Léontine, let's go, there's no more time to lose. That girl must explain her deception. She must tell us the truth.

(*HERMOCRATE leads LÉONTINE off to find Léonide. AGIS weeps.*)

Scene 9

AGIS. (*Through his tears.*) I have no hope.

(*LÉONIDE enters slowly and quietly, looking after Hermocrate and Léontine.*)

LÉONIDE. So they're gone, the meddlers. (*Seeing Agis.*) Agis, what is it?

(*AGIS pulls away from her.*)

LÉONIDE. Why won't you look at me?

AGIS. (*Furious.*) Why did you *come* here? Which of the three of us do you really intend to marry? Hermocrate? Léontine? Or is it me?

LÉONIDE. (*Gravely.*) Oh I see ... I have been found out.

AGIS. Don't you have a portrait for *me*—like the others?

LÉONIDE. I wouldn't have given the others my portrait if I hadn't intended to give you my life.

AGIS. *Hermocrate* can have your life! Or Léontine! Goodbye, I am leaving. You have been ... worse than false ... *cruel* ... I don't even know what to call it! Goodbye forever. You have killed me!

(*AGIS starts to leave. LÉONIDE catches him.*)

LÉONIDE. Wait! Listen to me!

AGIS. Don't *touch* me ! Let me go!

LÉONIDE. I will not let you go, I will never let you go. If you refuse to listen to me, you are the most ungrateful of men.

AGIS. Me, whom you deceived? *Ungrateful*?

LÉONIDE. But I did it for *you*, it was for *you* that I deceived everyone. I had to. Every false word I have spoken is proof of my love. My heart's desire is honest. My love is true. You're wrong to insult me. And all the love you have for me—you can't see that now, but you *do* love me. And you will respect me. You will even ask my forgiveness. I *know* I will get through to you!

AGIS. I just can't understand how ...

LÉONIDE. I did anything and everything I could to mislead them, to delude them, to seduce them. Because making them love me was the only way I could get to you, and you were the *only* object of everything I have done here. I was inspired at every turn by your eyes, your hands ... your mouth ...

AGIS. Ah, Aspasie, can I believe you?

LÉONIDE. Harlequin and Dimas helped me, they know my secret, they will confirm what I'm telling you. Ask them. I would even trust *them* to tell the truth about this!

AGIS. (*Still confused.*) Can it be possible that you are telling the truth? Aspasie .... It was for love of *me*?

LÉONIDE. Yes. But that isn't everything.

(*SHE pauses to gather her strength.*)

LÉONIDE. The princess you just called your enemy and mine ...

AGIS. Aspasie, if you *do* really love me you must know that she is trying to kill me. She will not spare the son of Cleomenes.

LÉONIDE. (*Urgently.*) I know who you are. (*A beat.*) And I am in a position to put *her* fate in *your* hands.

AGIS. But I am asking only that we be allowed to decide our *own* fate.

LÉONIDE. (*Interrupting him urgently.*) Listen to me! Her fate *is* in your hands.

(SHE turns to face Agis. Her hand moves to her heart.)

LÉONIDE. The love in her heart ... here ... puts her at your mercy.

AGIS. Her heart ...

(HE realizes.)

AGIS. You are Léonide, madam.

LÉONIDE. I told you before that you didn't yet know how much I love you. Now you do. You have all my secrets and all my love. All my life.

(AGIS, moved, falls to his knees at her feet. THEY both cry. HERMOCRATE and LÉONTINE enter.)

Scene 10 and Finale

HERMOCRATE. What is this? Agis on his knees?

(HE approaches Léonide and produces the portrait she gave him.)

HERMOCRATE. Of whom is this a portrait?
LÉONIDE. Of me.
LÉONTINE. (*Producing hers.*) And this one—you *impostor?*
LÉONIDE. That's me, too. Would you like me to take them back, and return yours?
HERMOCRATE. (*Interrupting her.*) Stop it! I think your jest has gone far enough. Who *are* you? Why did you come here?

(HERMOCRATE stands facing Léonide. Enter CORINE, followed by HARLEQUIN and DIMAS.)

LÉONIDE. I will tell you, but first ... Corine?
DIMAS. (*Entering.*) Master, did you see? Horses! Soldiers! There's a gilded carriage at the bottom of the garden!
CORINE. Madam, Ariston has arrived.
LÉONIDE. (*To Agis.*) Come, Sire. Come, accept the tributes of your subjects. The royal guard awaits your word. It is time to go.

(AGIS kisses Léontine and Hermocrate goodbye. LÉONIDE gives money to CORINE, who pays Dimas, then Harlequin. AGIS rejoins Léonide.)

LÉONIDE. You, Hermocrate, and you, Léontine, who at first denied me your support—perhaps you are beginning to see the truth through my deception. I came here to return the throne to Agis. And to give him my heart as well. If I had come as a woman, as myself, I might have lost him forever. If I hadn't deceived the two of you, it all might have come to nothing. I had to be sure, you see.

Hermocrate, you are certainly not to be pitied. I leave your reason in care of your heart.

And you, Léontine. When I made love to you, I kindled something in you. Now that you know who I am, I expect that fire has died out. (*A beat.*) Or am I wrong?

(LÉONIDE smiles at Hermocrate and Léontine, then leaves with AGIS. CORINE follows, HARLEQUIN and DIMAS move away. HERMOCRATE and LÉONTINE remain onstage, each standing alone.)

FADE TO BLACK

PRODUCTION NOTES

This play can of course be set in any period, or imagined in any way the production team finds most apt. The first production of this adaptation was set in 1730s France. These suggestions are based on that production. (Picture research is recommended.)

SETTINGS

The play is set in a garden. The deck was slightly raked, treated to look like a real outdoor ground surface—a partly abandoned section of a large formal garden. The wing and backdrop pieces, painted à la Watteau, combined references to an eighteenth-century theater with a sense of an actual garden. The show portal was ornately carved, gilt, covered with vines. The only furniture was one wooden bench.

COSTUMES

LÉONIDE
She is dressed as a man. Her appearance must be very elegant, but subtly so, and quite sober, so that she will fit in in Hermocrate's household. Sober silhouette, dark color, restrained pattern, extremely fine fabric, as befits a princess.

CORINE
She is also dressed as a man and also must be elegant and reasonably subdued. Possibly rustic colors, probably simpler fabrics and pattern(s) than Léonide. Corine might be tied in color and perhaps pattern to Harlequin.

HERMOCRATE

He is dressed simply and severely but with elegance, as befits a man devoted to study and contemplation who is also the guardian of the true prince. Plain silhouette, dark color (black is excellent), unshowy fabric, perhaps no pattern.

LÉONTINE

She is her brother's keeper and follower, so the same details of pattern might apply to her, at least at first. She might have a second costume, a bit more traditionally feminine, softer of silhouette and richer in fabric and color, for the scenes following her capitulation to Léonide/Phocion.

AGIS

He is at first utterly naive and clothed in fine fabrics beautifully tailored as becomes a prince. Plain silhouette, unshowy fabric, sober color, subdued pattern (if any). His costume might come undone as he becomes gradually undone by love: looser, even open at the neck, more buttons unbuttoned generally, perhaps down to his shirtsleeves by the end.

HARLEQUIN

He is the classic *commedia dell'arte* figure—with his diamond-patterned, belted costume, black mask, baton/joy stick and rough tricorn hat. Rustic colors (e.g. ochre, maroon), linens and cottons, roomy enough to accomodate possible acrobatic moves.

DIMAS

An old-timer at work in the garden. Simple cottons, linens and perhaps leather, rustic colors, all very lived-in.

PROPERTIES

4 PORTRAITS

Small enough to be pocketed or otherwise hidden, easily accessible in costumes of Léonide, Hermocrate and Léontine. The portraits are of Hermocrate, Léontine and Leonide's male and female aliases— Phocion and Aspasie.

SMALL COIN SACKS CONTAINING COINS

Sacks leather, silk or linen, easily accessible in Léonide's costume, easily tucked away in Harlequin's and Dimas'. Coins burnished gold, weighty in the palm of the hand, should clink easily.

CORINE'S PAINTING MATERIALS

Could be carried in a leather satchel. Collapsible easel fitted to hold the portraits just below Corine's eye level. Small brushes, sketching pencils, feather pens— all in a small container. Small water container of copper, tin or dark glass. Sizeable seashell serving as her palette, with green, yellow, white, gray and black paint daubs on it.

DIMAS' GARDENING TOOLS AND EQUIPMENT

HARLEQUIN'S BATON/JOY STICK

About 15 inches long, easily reached for and returned to his belt (see *commedia dell' arte* prints for research).

ROYAL INSIGNIA AND BOX

Perhaps a gold or bronze medallion on a rich, wide ribbon, produced from a fine box and placed around Agis' neck by Léonide at the end of the play.

Other Publications For Your Interest

RAVENSCROFT. (Little Theatre.) Mystery. Don Nigro. 1m., 5f. Simple unit set. This unusual play is several cuts above the genre it explores, a Gothic thriller for groups that don't usually do such things, a thinking person's mystery, a dark comedy that is at times immensely funny and at others quite frightening. On a snowy night, Inspector Ruffing is called to a remote English country house to investigate the headlong plunge of a young manservant, Patrick Roarke, down the main staircase, and finds himself getting increasingly involved in the lives of five alluring and dangerous women—Marcy, the beautiful Viennese governess with a past, Mrs. Ravenscroft, the flirtatious and chattery lady of the manor, Gillian, her charming but possibly demented daughter, Mrs. French, the formidable and passionate cook, and Dolly, a frantic and terrified little maid—who lead him through an increasingly bewildering labyrinth of contradictory versions of what happened to Patrick and to the dead Mr. Ravenscroft before him. There are ghosts at the top of the staircase, skeletons in the closet, and much more than the Inspector had bargained for as his quest to solve one mystery leads him deeper and deeper into others and to an investigation of his own tortured soul and the nature of truth itself. You will not guess the ending, but you will be teased, seduced, bewildered, amused, frightened and led along with the Inspector to a dark encounter with truth, or something even stranger. A funny, first rate psychological mystery, and more.

(#19987)

DARK SONNETS OF THE LADY, THE. (Advanced Groups.) Drama. Don Nigro. 4m., 4f. Unit set. First produced professionally at the McCarter Theatre in Princeton and a finalist for the National Play Award, this stunningly theatrical and very funny drama takes place in Vienna in the fall of the year 1900, when Dora, a beautiful and brilliant young girl, walks into the office of Sigmund Freud, then an obscure doctor in his forties, to begin the most famous and controversial encounter in the history of psychoanalysis. Dora is funny, suspicious, sarcastic and elusive, and Freud become fascinated and obsessed by her and by the intricate labyrinth of her illness. He moves like a detective through the mystery of her life, and we meet in the course of his journey through her mind: her lecherous father, her obsessively house-cleaning mother, her irritating brother, her sinister admirer Herr Klippstein and his sensual and seductive wife, and their pretty and lost little governess. Nightmares, fantasies, hallucinations and memories all come alive onstage in a wild kaleidoscopic tapestry as Freud moves closer and closer to the truth about Dora's murky past, and the play becomes a kind of war between the two of them about what the truth is, about the uneasy truce between men and women, and ultimately a tragic love story. Laced throughout with eerie and haunting Strauss waltzes, this is a rich, complex, challenging and delightfully intriguing universe, a series of riddles one inside the other that lead the audience step by step to the center of Dora's troubled soul and her innermost secrets. Is Dora sick, or is the corrupt patriarchal society in which she and Freud are both trapped the real source of a complex group neurosis that binds all the characters together in a dark web of desperate erotic relationships, a kind of beautiful, insane and terrible dance of life, desire and death? (#5952)

PICTURE OF DORIAN GRAY, THE (Little Theatre.) Drama. Adapted by John O... from the novel by Oscar Wilde... I Int. w/apron for other scenes. English playwright John Osborne (Look Back in Anger, Inadmissible Evidence, The Entertainer) has given us a brilliant dramatisation of Wilde's classic novel about a young man who, magically, retains his youth and beauty while the decay of advancing years and moral corruption only appears on a portrait painted by one of his lovers. Following the advice of the evil Lord Harry, a cynic who, fashionably, mocks any and all institutions and moral precepts, Dorian comes to believe that the only purpose of life is simply for one to realize, and glorify, one's own nature. In so doing, he is inevitably sucked into the maelstrom of degradation and despair, human nature being what it is. "Osborne has done much more than a scissors-and-paste job on Wilde's famous story. He has thinned out the over-abundant epigrams, he has highlighted the topical concept of youth as a commodity for which one would sell one's soul and he has, in Turn of the Screw fashion, created a sense of evil through implication. Osborne conveys moral disintegration through the gradual breakdown of the hero's language into terse, broken phrases and through a creeping phantasmagoria."—London, The Guardian. "What is so interesting about John Osborne's adaptation of The Picture of Dorian Gray is that he had found in Oscar Wilde's macabre morality a velveted barouche for his own favorite themes. Osborne funks none of the greenery-valley vulgarity of the fabulous story, and conveys much of its fascination."—London, Daily Telegraph. State author when ordering. **(#18954)**

FALL OF THE HOUSE OF USHER, THE. (Little Theatre.) Drama. Gip Hoppe. Music by Jay Hagenbuckle. 6m. 3f. Int. A comfortable suburban family man receives a desperate telephone call from an obscure and forgotten childhood acquaintance. Thus starts a journey into madness that will take Ed Allen to the House of Usher and the terrible secrets and temptations contained there. In this modern adaptation of the classic short story by Edgar Allen Poe, playwright Gip Hoppe takes Gothic horror into the 90s, questioning the definition of "sanity" in the same way Poe did in his day. Ed arrives to find Roderick in a state of panic and anxiety over the impending death of his sister, Madeline. As he tries to sort out the facts, he becomes tangled in a family web of incest and murder. Finding himself infatuated with the beautiful Madeline, his "outside life" fades from his memory as he descends to the depths of madness that inflict all the residents of The House of Usher. *The Fall of the House of Usher* is an exhilarating theatrical adventure leading to an apocalyptic ending that will have audiences thrilled. Actors and designers will be challenged in new ways in this unpredictable and wildly entertaining play. Cassette tape. Use of Mr. Hagenbuckle's music will greatly enhance the play, but it is not mandatory. **(#7991)**